Howard M. Wachtel

THE

MONEY

MANDARINS

The Making of a New Supranational Economic Order

PANTHEON BOOKS, New York

Library of Congress Cataloging-in-Publication Data

Wachtel, Howard M.
The Money mandarins.

 Bibliography: p.
 Includes index.
 1. Economic history—1945– . 2. International finance. 3. Dollar, American. 4. Foreign exchange problem—United States. 5. Monetary policy—United States. I. Title.
HC59.W23 1986   337′.09′048   85-28455
ISBN 0-394-54299-1

Book design by Jennifer Dossin
Manufactured in the United States of America

First Edition

To Marie, Elizabeth, and Sarah

CONTENTS

PREFACE

UBLIC fatigue with the welfare state and accidents of economic history, such as OPEC, are the prevailing explanations for the conservative revival in political economy and the liberal retreat. These analyses, however, do not provide convincing answers to the questions: why did the conservative restoration occur at all; why did it happen in the late 1970s and not before; and why did it appear in so many countries at roughly the same time?

The answers are found in the changes in the world economy that transformed the national political-economic debate in the 1970s. After 1973, there emerged what *Business Week* calls a "world of stateless money," which "has in turn bred a stateless banking system in which national boundaries mean very little. . . . Now international commerce is totally dependent on this new supranational banking system . . . that greases the path of money movements [but] also creates a vicious cycle of currency instability."[1] The key word is "supra-national." During the 1970s and 1980s, private commercial and banking interests began to operate supranationally, beyond the public policy and regulatory reach of national governments. They used this extraterritorial power to leverage public policy changes inside the United States.

This book is about the intersection of political-economic changes in the United States and the emergence of a new supranational economy; how the one influences the other. After an introductory chapter, which presents the argument of the book in very abbreviated form, there are three chapters in Part I on the historical background to the evolution of a supranational economy.

Chapter 2 contains material on the origins of the post–World War II Bretton Woods system, which structured the world economy for about a quarter of a century, and information on how a world economy functions. The politics of international money is examined in Chapter 3, followed in Chapter 4 by an analysis of the breakdown of Bretton Woods, as seen through some of the major political and economic events of the 1960s: the gold war between France and the United States, the war in Viet Nam, and, finally, Nixon's New Economic Policy.

Part II is about the evolution of the supranational economy and how it influences contemporary politics and economics. The emergence of *Business Week*'s "stateless money" as a force in the world economy is analyzed in Chapter 5, and the fallout from this development is the subject of the next two chapters: worldwide economic austerity (Chapter 6) and the changing character of the American corporation (Chapter 7). The last two chapters analyze how the supranational economy changed politics and economic policy in the United

States in the 1980s and how public policy should be reconstructed to correct the distortions in the economy caused by unregulated supranationalism.

A project of this scope and complexity is fraught with risks for an author. The subject is so large that one reader might say, "You have left this out," and another, "You have left that out of the story." Any important subject, however, is bound to be large and complex. Everything cannot be included or nothing will be understood —the forest-for-the-trees metaphor.

Tackling this particular large question presents more than the expected problems, because source material is limited. Bankers, who play such a large part in the story, are notoriously secretive, are reluctant to grant interviews, and have no tradition as memoirists, unlike generals or secretaries of state. Yet as Susan Strange, the British chronicler of sterling's fate after the war, commented: "Surely this is a subject just as deserving of a full record as the minor battles and parochial conflicts that are the subject of so many published memoirs."[2]

The three academic disciplines that could lay claim to this research terrain—economics, international relations, and political science—for the most part ignored the connections between changes in the world economy and domestic politics. Mainstream economics in the past several decades has accelerated its quest for the mathematical precision of abstract theory, abandoning its intellectual traditions of political economy. International relations and political science have never felt comfortable with the integration of economics into their body of knowledge, with a few notable exceptions that will be used in this book.

I am left with some academic writings and reading between the lines of official reports. The best source of information has been economic and financial journalists who have produced a rich body of factual and analytical material on the world economy. "Without press cuttings," as Susan Strange said about her study of the British role in the world economy, "this history could never have been written."[3]

ACKNOWLEDGMENTS

A T AN early stage in the development of this project, I received encouragement from Robert Lekachman, Lester Thurow, Paul Streeten, Cynthia Taft Morris, Ulf Himmelstrand, and Nancy Barrett. The book was written during a year's sabbatical in 1984–85 from The American University, which provided me the necessary time and financial support. While on sabbatical, I was an Academic Visitor at the London School of Economics, Department of International Relations. I am grateful to Professor Susan Strange for arranging this appointment, which enabled me to make full use of the library of the London School of Economics.

An American University summer research grant in 1983 provided the time to start research on the project, and travel funds from the Mellon Foundation grant to the College of Arts and Sciences of The American University expanded my opportunities for research. A grant from the Transnational Institute of the Institute for Policy Studies helped to free me from other obligations during my sabbatical year.

Different parts of the book were presented at two fellows' meetings of the Transnational Institute in Amsterdam in 1984 and 1985. Comments on my work at those meetings sharpened the ideas in the book. I particularly want to thank Robert Borosage and John Cavanagh of the Institute for Policy Studies for their support, encouragement, and critical comments.

Marie Tyler-McGraw read the entire manuscript and offered meticulous comments on the substance and presentation of the ideas in the book. A conversation with Wynne Godley forced me to think carefully about the policy implications of the themes I was developing. Comments on the entire manuscript were provided by Jon Wisman, Elliot Schwartz, Hugo Radice, John Willoughby, and Andre Gunder Frank. I thank these colleagues without implicating them in any way in the final product.

Ron Goldfarb represented me as legal counsel on the book contract. Typing in London was by Textpertise, whose proprietors are Madeline and Joost Cohen. In the United States, typing was done by Nancy Smith.

To James Peck, senior editor at Pantheon Books, I am indebted for doing what an editor is supposed to do: encourage, criticize, and improve the presentation of the ideas in the book. Finally, I acknowledge the patient confidence that André Schiffrin, managing director of Pantheon Books, provided at critical stages in the development of the book.

THE MONEY MANDARINS

1

WAYS OF
THINKING ABOUT THE
SUPRANATIONAL ECONOMY

E LECT a left-of-center government and the economy becomes a mess, according to today's conventional wisdom. This perception spread through the industrial democracies after OPEC appeared on the scene and drove up oil prices in the early 1970s. When the economy ceased delivering the goods at reasonable prices and long gas lines replaced easy access to the fuel that powered its automobiles, the public became disillusioned with the postwar liberal economic nostrums that relied on government policy to promote economic welfare.

Government is an identifiable target, with names and faces, and it was blamed for all that ailed the economy in the 1970s. Economic regulation was no longer seen as protection for the common good but instead became a public nuisance that hindered economic growth. The corporate system, which only a few years earlier had been in disrepute, suddenly became an economic knight on a white horse. The Republican party was resuscitated and became identified with economic modernization in the 1980s, leaving behind the Hoover albatross that it had been carrying around for nearly half a century. The political mood has changed, and a new conservatism now boasts about becoming more than a transitory phenomenon.

The conservative response to the economic dislocation of the 1970s has found a receptive audience. Restore the rule of private capital and permit markets to perform their historic function of weeding out the inefficient (read "weak") and rewarding the efficient (read "strong"). Neoconservatives have resurrected a nineteenth-century metaphysical concept of the "free market," as a substitute for the pragmatic mixed economy of the mid-twentieth century. We have become travelers in a time machine that transports us back to an earlier ideological time and place. As public policy attempts to re-create an economic utopia built around the free market, economic privatization, and limited government, the common good is no longer an idea that excites our collective imagination.

Nothing reveals the magnitude of these sea changes in national politics more than the television image of Senator Barry Goldwater standing before the 1984 Republican Convention repeating his "extremism in defense of liberty" to the cheers of his conservative followers. Twenty years earlier, this same phrase was received differently, as the television networks showed by fading from one to the other. The senator's squared-off, Dick Tracy jaw was characteristically thrust forward in both frames. But in 1984 there was the confidence that only comes with "I told you so."

The present dilemma of liberal democracy can be traced back to the changes in the world economy that occurred between 1971 and 1973. Those years marked the end of the postwar international arrangements that governed the world economy known as the Bretton Woods system. After 1973, international money was deregulated, currencies fluctuated in value with each other, and the international dimension of private banking acquired an unprecedented degree of power and influence. All this occurred with little public regulation, and the consequent result has been international monetary instability—world debt, high interest rates, bank failures, and inflation. The shift in political economy away from the liberal-centrist consensus of the 1960s toward a conservative-right revival in the 1980s was in large part caused by destabilizing changes in the world economy.

A new breed of money mandarins has thrived in a 1980s atmosphere of deregulated high-stakes global finance. Aided by a revolution in information and communications technology, private bankers now preside over an integrated network of global finance, leapfrogging national boundaries in the same way as the communications satellite which recognizes no borders. The corporation has become dominated by financial wizards who know little about production but everything about leveraged buyouts and takeover strategies. In government, policy makers, trained to deal with the real problems of employment, economic growth, and productivity, have been swept aside and replaced by officials from the Federal Reserve and Treasury departments whose expertise is in money and finance. Public money mandarins, therefore, comport with their private counterparts in banks and corporations to govern the symbols of a world economy, while real human needs are neglected.

Supranationalism: First Impressions

O N OCTOBER 6, 1979, Paul Volcker, chairman of the Federal Reserve Board, set the American economy on a road to monetary austerity that led to the most severe recession in the United States since the Great Depression. By Christmas 1980, the prime rate of interest—that rate charged by the major U.S. banks to their most credit-worthy customers— soared to an historic peak of 21.5 percent. The measured unemployment rate reached double digits for the first time after World War II in September of 1982, and before the recession was over, it hit the 11 percent mark, a post–Great Depression record.[1]

Volcker introduced monetary austerity in response to successive international runs on the dollar in 1977 and 1979 that threatened to turn worldwide speculation against a weak dollar into a free fall in its value. World monetary events that are beyond the regulatory reach of the United States government forced economic austerity measures on the country in the late 1970s. In the early 1980s, the country faced the other side of this coin, an overvaluation of the dollar that makes U.S. exports too expensive in the world economy and erodes America's industrial-manufacturing base.

The international monetary system was, by 1979, a *supranational* monetary order. Private international banks, and the unregulated growth of the private money they control (Eurodollars), began to function outside of the monetary safeguards created during the 1930s. "There isn't a nation in the world," said Senator Hubert Humphrey in 1978, "which controls even the central symbol of independence—the value of its money. Inflation, recession, and stagflation are global in nature."[2]

A new international monetary order is one feature of the supranational economy. Another is the changing character of the American corporation. The corporation today is more a center for financial gamesmanship and less a locus of production. The American corporation operates supranationally, by extending its labor market worldwide and conducting more of its productive activity outside of the United States. "Their basic aim," says *Business Week* magazine about the supranational corporations, "is to maximize worldwide profits, without regard to source of product or national boundaries."[3] The supranational economy, therefore, consists of banks and corporations that conduct their economic affairs beyond the political reach of national governments, which are confined to specific geographic boundaries.

Between 1980 and 1984, investment abroad by American companies was over $200 billion, amounting to eleven out of every one hundred dollars invested by American firms in those years.[4] The supranational enterprise sells back to the United States not just a product from its investment in other countries; increasingly, it tries to sell the United States an economic and social policy imported from countries such as South Korea, Chile, and Singapore. Labor restrictions and regulatory relief are the two political products most often offered to the United States by supranational corporations that seek to escape policies developed over the last half century in the United States.

Anaconda, Montana, was the company town in which Anaconda Copper smelted ore that was mined twenty-eight miles down the road in Butte, Montana. On a September morning in 1980, the fifteen hundred employees of Anaconda learned that their jobs no longer existed because the company claimed it could not afford the cost of regulatory compliance. Instead, they announced that the copper ore would be shipped to Japan, smelted there, and sold back to the United States. Anaconda, a giant company in its own right, had recently been acquired in a merger by a bigger corporate conglomerate, Arco Oil.

Anaconda is not just importing refined copper into the United States from Japan, a curiosity in itself, because this type of intracompany "import" from an American corporation is listed without differentiation alongside an import of a Toyota car in U.S. economic accounts. Anaconda Copper and its parent, Arco Oil, were behaving like true supranationals, trying to circumvent established legislative procedures by an end run, then using their worldwide productive base to leverage policy changes in the United States. "They have used the closing as a political tool, to send a message to Congress about the Clean Air Act," complains Steve Rovig, who is on the staff of Senator Max Baucus (D-Montana).[5]

This illustrates the conflict between the public policy responsibility of a government, bounded by geography, and the private supranational world of corporations and banks that do not recognize any geographic limits on their activities. Richard Barnet and Ronald Muller, whose book, *Global Reach*, stimulated an entire genre of work on the subject, put the thesis this way: "The men who run the global corporations are the first in history with the organization, technology, money, and ideology to make a credible try at managing the world as an integrated economic unit. . . . What they are demanding in essence is the right to transcend the nation-state, and in the process, transform it."[6]

The growth of a supranational economic order, in both its monetary and production dimensions, has contributed to international economic instability and made inflation and unemployment worse. As the world economy fluctuates, so does each person's economic well-being. Instability in the dollar's value contributes to inflation in the United States, as importers and exporters hedge their uncertainty about the future by adding a cost to their products. Lower wage rates and regulatory permissiveness in other countries reduce the number of jobs in the United States. A strong dollar, due to high U.S. interest rates, has the same effect on American jobs; exports become more expensive abroad while foreign imports are cheaper for the American consumer. A weakening dollar, on the other hand, forces the government to raise interest rates in the United States to strengthen the value of the dollar abroad.

Supranational American corporations and banks are concerned for their own interests in the world economy with results that are at times detrimental to the larger public economic interest of the United States. Unregulated, private, economic supranationalism challenges the nation-state and its public-policy-making authority. The dilemmas caused by these structural changes in the world economy have produced a public discussion that has so far dealt more with symptoms and palliatives than with causes and remedies. What is not known about these global zero-sum games is where they came from and what can be done to move back to a positive-sum game by changing the economic rule book, both in terms of national economic policies and a transformed world economic order.

If the world economy does not become more stable, it will continue to lurch from one global economic crisis to another—either a debt default, or a free fall in the dollar, or an overvalued dollar—and the United States will continue to distort its economy with monetarist austerity. The reconstruction of a political-economic agenda that restores stable economic growth and provides the basis for economic justice requires an understanding of what went wrong in the world economy in the 1970s and 1980s and what can be done to reverse this process.

Retreat from the Liberal Consensus

I N THE middle of the twentieth century, there was a general consensus on economic and social policy in the industrialized democracies. Government was committed to intervene in the economy to seek high levels of employment while much social policy was designed to aid those individuals who fell outside of the mainstream employment system. Whether the U.S. government was dominated by Democrats or Republicans dictated the content of political rhetoric and how aggressively these commitments were pursued. But the policies were never fundamentally challenged. A Republican president, Richard M. Nixon, for example, presided over some of the most far-reaching interventionist policies. He is the only president to impose wage and price controls in a peacetime economy, and many of the regulatory policies that are now being reversed were passed during his administration. Nixon proclaimed in 1971: "We are all Keynesians now." This changed in the 1980s.

Support for Keynesian employment strategies and social welfare policies has dissipated since the early 1970s. This development has been examined by political economists from two perspectives. One group locates the source of the problem in the misguided public policies of the modern nation-state by assuming it operates as a self-contained economic entity.[7] Another group identifies the cause as the changing international economic relationships among sovereign nation-states.[8] One aspect missing from these explanations is the realization that the world economy today is a supranational economy, where production and banking transcend the narrow public policy boundaries of the nation-state and function outside the traditional rules of international economic relationships among countries.

This conflict between the sovereign power of the nation-state and the supranational reach of private economic interests is not new. What is new is the contemporary form of the conflict. The rules of the global economic game changed between 1971 and 1973 when the postwar monetary system, known as Bretton Woods, collapsed of its own weight. In its place was substituted a substantially deregulated world monetary order. J. W. Anderson of the *Washington Post* notes that the "world has not yet adequately adjusted" to these changes in the world economy that link "each country's movements more closely to other countries', making purely national policies harder and more expensive to carry out when they are not in harmony with international trends."[9]

Global Economic Interdependence

W E STILL see ourselves in the United States as an island nation surrounded on the east and west by great oceans and to the north and south by friendly neighbors. The economic reality is different, however. More than 20 percent of industrial production is exported, accounting for one out of every six manufacturing jobs. Two of every five acres of agricultural land are used for export. About one-third of all corporate prof-its derives either from exports or foreign investments.[10]

American international banks have entangled each one of us in global financial affairs, whether or not we choose to be. About fifteen hundred banks throughout the United States are part of Third World loan syndi-cates put together by the major international banks. Part of each deposit we make is at risk in these Third World loans, as it would be with any other. But it is the enormous size and concentration that makes the differ-ence. About $550 billion were owed in 1984 to private U.S. banks by Third World and East European countries whose ability to repay these loans is periodically in doubt.[11]

Nothing made American dependence on economic de-cisions taken at remote foreign locations more graphic than OPEC, an organization that the rest of the world barely noticed when it was formed in obscurity in the early 1960s. By 1973, however, OPEC had become transformed into the most powerful economic actor on the world stage. In 1970, a barrel of crude oil sold for $1.80, the price of a breakfast of bacon, eggs, and cof-fee. During the October 1973 Middle East war, the price of a barrel of oil was increased and reached a plateau by March 1974 that was about two and one-half times higher than before the war, the price of a moderately expensive lunch. The fall of the shah of Iran drove the price of oil up another two and one-half times to a peak of $34 per barrel, and in the 1980s it settled in at about $30 per barrel. This is the cost of an expensive dinner. Prior to this run-up in oil prices, the U.S. had to pro-duce a half bushel of wheat for one barrel of oil; today, the United States has to produce ten bushels of wheat to exchange for one barrel of oil.[12]

These global economic developments tied the Carter administration into knots and contributed to the discrediting of liberal economic and social policies. Hindsight has afforded C. Fred Bergsten, the man in charge of international economic policy in Carter's Treasury Department, a strategic perspective that was missing from the administration's policies. "The United States," he says, "has simultaneously become much more dependent on the world economy and much less able to dictate the course of international economic events. . . . Private entities, often operating outside the direct control of any government, have reduced sovereign power in general and that of the United States in particular."[13]

The Conservative Restoration

F OR THE most part, governments adopted a laissez-faire policy attitude toward these massive upheavals in the world economy. If the question was asked in 1971 about how the world would adapt in a decade to the end of fixed exchange rates (the cornerstone of the postwar Bretton Woods economic system), the growth of Eurodollars to over 1 trillion, world debt reaching 700 billions of dollars, crude oil prices fifteen times higher, interest rates around 13 percent, unemployment rates throughout the industrial world of over 10 percent, and inflation reaching double digits, the answer would be that such things were impossible. But the U.S. economy has adjusted to these transformations.

Other questions might also be asked, however. For example, could the pain of adjustment have been eased, made more equitable, and the changes have been managed without permitting private supranational economic forces to reach such a pinnacle of power? And what about the future? Has the United States simply bought a little time before the unattended problems of the 1970s become the destabilizing forces of the late 1980s? In presenting the issue this way, something can be learned as well about the equally important changes in domestic politics, from a consensus built around centrist, Keynesian social welfare policies to a conservative political economy of monetarism and privatization.

If I had written in 1971 that the United States and Great Britain would be governed in the 1980s by parties that seek to re-create a nineteenth-century free-market utopia, no one would have paid much attention to the words because they would not have stood the test of the marketplace of ideas. But that is the governing philosophy of these two great industrial democracies, implemented through monetarism, a retreat from governmental responsibility for the public's welfare, and a restoration of unregulated private commercial interests. Nor is this occurring just in England and the United States. In one form or another, these ideas have blown through central and northern Europe, although with less of a gale force.

Only in the Mediterranean rim of Spain, Portugal, France, Italy, and Greece has there been an exemption from the conservative political tide. In part, this can be explained by the fact that some of these countries (Italy and France excepted) were recovering from years of authoritarian rightist governments, and the people wanted a change. These smaller countries, however, have not been able to implement their socialist economic visions because of the austere world economic environment in which they have tried to create political-economic change in their countries. Commenting on France, Michael Dobbs of the *Washington Post* characterizes the shift in Mitterrand's policies as putting "pragmatism above ideology, credibility above compassion," in order to "remain in power."[14] The conservative ideological restoration is becoming the new consensus, just as the liberal Keynesian one dominated the first quarter century after World War II.

When the U.S. government's promise to stabilize the economy could not be fulfilled, with oil prices, inflation, unemployment, the value of the dollar, and interest rates gyrating wildly out of control, political attitudes tilted away from the mixed economy toward the only apparent alternative: private corporate and banking control. In the words of Morton M. Kondracke, executive editor of the *New Republic* magazine, "The country . . .decided to try recapturing control by turning to basic American devices, John Wayne devices—private enterprise, individualism, the free market, military strength and interventionism overseas."[15]

The specific policy measures needed to create such a restoration of private influence were deregulation, tax cuts at the upper ends of the income distribution that left more money in private investment hands, and monetarist economic policies in place of Keynesian economic management. "Ever since the Depression," writes the economic journalist Robert J. Samuelson, "capitalism's division of labor has been this: Business would create greater material wealth, while government would rub out insecurity."[16] In the late 1960s and early 1970s, the public questioned the value of the former, and in the late 1970s and early 1980s, it has begun to doubt the possibility of the latter.

The Supranational Economy and Its Antecedents

OLICY makers see the world economy divided into two parts. The first is private market-regulated competition among corporations and banks based in different countries. The second involves public relationships among nation-states governed by international public rules. The supranational economy, however, increasingly dominates the commanding heights of the world economy, and it is distinct from this traditional way of thinking about the international economy. In the ungoverned supranational economy, private commercial, financial, and communications enterprises circumvent both domestic public regulation and international public rules by operating outside of the regulatory reach of governments. The supranationals pursue their own global strategic interests, which can be at odds with the national interests of their countries of origin. The end product is a system of world economic governance with parameters defined by the unregulated market and rules administered by supranational banks and corporations.

The more familiar term used to describe the modern commercial enterprise in the world economy is "multinational" or "transnational." Neither, however, captures the essence of the evolution of private global economic interests in the late 1970s and 1980s. "Multinational" refers to enterprises operating in many nations; "transnational" conjures up an image of firms operating across national boundaries. "Supranational" embraces both of these images but is preferable because it means that private interests can operate beyond the boundaries of national governments, thereby escaping national policies, while at the same time the supranationals use their influence to leverage policy changes in their home governments.

The rise of the supranational economy feeds into an increase in political nationalism and contributes to a breakdown in international political collaboration. The economist Robert Heilbroner speaks of an "ill-understood confrontation between political power, which is growing at the national level, and economic power, which is growing at the supranational level."[17] Supranationalism weakens the nation-state's ability to control its own economic destiny, and this produces a public impatience with other countries that reveals itself in a growing political nationalism and support for protectionist economic policies.

The Emergence of a Supranational Economy

T wo important changes occurred in the 1970s that expedited the development of a supranational economic order. The first was the decision to deregulate the international monetary system between 1971 and 1973, following the collapse of the postwar Bretton Woods arrangements. The second was a communications and information revolution that transformed banking and money.

The End of Bretton Woods
Prior to 1971, there were public rules governing international monetary affairs. From 1973 onward, however, the world economy has functioned with fewer public

rules and regulations. International monetary affairs were the first experiment with deregulation, an idea that found its political audience a decade later. The decision to experiment with the deregulation of international money was, however, both bold and risky.

The dollar took on additional burdens after 1973 because of OPEC price hikes for crude oil. Dollars not only circulate in the United States; they are also used in the world economy in support of international trade. Known as Eurodollars, this form of stateless money is controlled solely by private banking interests with little monitoring or regulation either by the United States government or by any other international authority. The protections American citizens have come to expect for their money in the banking system do not apply to Eurodollars. Prior to the collapse of Bretton Woods, Eurodollars were a tiny blip on the monetary screen. By the early 1980s, however, they had grown to over $1 trillion, about three times as large as the domestic money supply.

A world economic order emerged in the 1970s fashioned by private commercial and banking interests in pursuit of global profits wherever they arose and with whatever consequences for public policy. Paul Streeten, a longtime student of multinational corporations, laments the "resistance to global action on the part of governments," which he contrasts with the "successful coordination of international action by big business— by the transnational corporations and by banks in the Eurocurrency market."[18] Government's proper role is not to manage private affairs but to establish a small number of relatively simple principles to guide the pursuit of private interests. This view is shared by the Brazilian economist Celso Furtado—one of the creators of Third World dependency theory in the 1960s. He points out that the "aim is not so much to curb transnationalization as to subject it to economic policy objectives formulated at the national or international level."[19]

The Information and Communications Revolution

Instantaneous electronic communication via satellite enables vast sums of money to be moved anywhere in the world in a matter of seconds. This fuels speculative movements of money and raises the stakes in international finance. Rumors—whether well founded or not—run through financial trading rooms without the intervals of time needed to quiet them. Time, the great equalizer in financial speculation, enables rational thought to replace reflexive action. But with time now reduced to a fraction of a second, it no longer provides that protective space.

This is what occurred in the case of Continental Illinois National Bank in the spring of 1984, when rumors about its inability to collect on defaulted loans ran through the international financial community like a prairie fire. In a matter of hours, billions of dollars were withdrawn from Continental Illinois, and the nation's eighth largest bank was near bankruptcy until a $7.5 billion rescue package from the federal government was assembled. In this instance, technology had disarmed the best defense against speculative rumors, and funds from the public treasury were substituted for time as protection against a financial crisis.

A peek inside an international currency trading room is like entering the situation room at the Pentagon. High-level strategists mingle with their operatives, who sit before a bank of telephones, fitted with automatic dialing devices, which enable the money movers to reach some forty different locations around the world with just the punch of a button on the telephone console. Dozens of computer screens throw off a green light that competes with the fluorescents overhead for illumination. David Edwards, a former trader for Citibank, has been inside some sixty such financial trading rooms in both the United States and Europe, and he provides a unique firsthand account of this new financial wizardry. He describes these movers and shakers of international finance as "street fighters, accustomed to thinking on their feet, making as many as 50 decisions a day about more money than 100 executives earn in their lifetimes."[20] In the trading rooms of the City—London's financial district, which can claim the largest concentration of international financial trading rooms—Cockney accents are more likely to be heard than are those from Oxford or Cambridge.

Against this arsenal of technology and global finance, the sluggish regulatory influence of the nation-state has become an anachronism. The *Economist* pointed this out in its 1984 "Survey of International Banking": "Sophisticated information systems and the resulting internationalization of the world's capital markets have made artificial domestic restraints less and less tenable."[21] The American financial watchdogs have been caught off guard by every important development in international finance in recent years. The reason for this is to be found in the technological revolution in communications that has reduced the time between transactions and has enabled supranational financial enterprises to extend their money dealings to virtually every corner of the globe. The sun never sets on these financial trading empires. Countries from every time zone on the earth have their moment on the computer screen.

Liberal economists, in the current usage of that term, have ignored these important global financial developments, because their doctrine confines money and finance to the secondary role of a lubricant that aids the circuit of production and employment. The real economy of production, investment, and consumption is dominant according to this view, and what Peter F.

Drucker, the contemporary guru of business philosophy, calls the "symbol economy of money and credit" is derivative. "The 'real economy' controls," he says in describing the liberal point of view, and "money is only the 'veil of things.' "[22] Liberals have ceded the monetary policy terrain to conservative monetarist economists who have always seen the symbol economy driving the real economy. In today's supranational world of global finance, however, this has to be reconsidered if an employment and growth strategy for economic renewal is to succeed.

Public Policy and the Supranational Economy

P OLITICS and public policy have not yet come to terms with the supranational economic order. While economic affairs are increasingly supranational, government remains confined to its political boundaries. International political cooperation has diminished at a time when it needs to become stronger. The revolt against government has left the public with weaker protections against the fallout from the supranational economy. With fewer policy tools at their command and with diminished legitimacy, governments are less able to define and protect the common good. Instead, they are left with the mop-up operation after some failure of the supranational economy threatens to further destabilize a fragile world economic order, as with the instances of private bank bailouts that occurred with increasing regularity in the 1980s.

Paul Streeten framed the problem this way: "There is a gap between the degree of economic, social and cultural interdependence created by the rapid advances in the technology of communications and transport, and the institutional responses to these advances."[23] The emerging supranational economic order requires new policy instruments in the domestic economy that are integrated with new institutional structures in the international economy. This point is echoed by the *Washington Post* columnist J. W. Anderson: "When the authoritative work on the economics of the 1960s and 1970s finally appears, the systematic neglect of international realities will . . . be central to the explanation of what went wrong."[24]

The United States must come to terms with the reality of relative commercial parity in the world economy. No longer is the U.S. pre-eminent, but it acts as if it is, or at least wants to be. While America still holds virtually all of the monetary cards, the commercial card game is being played with a different deck. In the face of these transformations in the world economy, the Republicans are living a mid-nineteenth-century nostalgia and the Democrats a mid-twentieth-century nostalgia. Neither one is living in the last fifth of the twentieth century, preparing the international institutional infrastructure for the next century.

This is the first reason for a change in the way the rules of the games are defined and enforced in the world economy. A second is derived from the fact that the conglomeration of nation-states in the world is no match for the transnational global reach of supranational corporations and banks. International public policy must address these new supranational commercial and monetary conditions. "The gap of our times is not so much . . . that between science and morality, as that between the soaring technological imagination and the inert institutional imagination."[25]

I

The

Bretton Woods

System:

PAX AMERICANA ECONOMICA, 1946–1971

2

BRETTON WOODS, 1944

T HE Bretton Woods system is the unlikely name given to the set of rules that governed the world economy for twenty-five years after World War II. The name is taken from the New Hampshire resort town that backs onto the Presidential Range of the White Mountains, where some 730 delegates and participants from forty-four countries met in July 1944 to establish the governance of the postwar international economy. "For maybe 100 years, there have been monetary conferences of one kind or other," reminisced Edward Bernstein, the executive secretary of the U.S. delegation at the 1944 conference, during a fortieth anniversary conference held at the same hotel in Bretton Woods. "But the one we had here 40 years ago was the only one that ever accomplished anything."[1]

The International Monetary Fund (IMF) and the World Bank were created at the Bretton Woods conference, along with a system of rules that governed the world economy for a quarter of a century. Most important among these rules was the establishment of fixed rates of exchange among currencies—the value of one nation's currency in terms of other nations' currencies—and the mechanism that permitted these values to be altered. The surviving industrial market economies—primarily the United States and Great Britain—made a commitment to raise capital for the reconstruction of those allied countries whose economies had been destroyed by the war.

The Bretton Woods conference did not occur on the spur of the moment in 1944 as an instinctive response to the need to restructure the world economy after the war. A week after Pearl Harbor, President Franklin D. Roosevelt set in motion a process that was to lead to New Hampshire two and one-half years later. The secretary of the treasury, Henry Morgenthau, Jr., took the lead. On December 14, 1941, he asked Harry Dexter White "to think about . . . and plan for setting up an 'Inter-Allied Stabilization Fund' " that would "provide the basis for post-war international monetary stabilization arrangements; and to provide a post-war 'international currency.' "[2] In the intervening years, there were discussions, memos, working drafts, and negotiations, primarily between the United States and Great Britain, over the structure of the postwar world economic order.

Between Pearl Harbor and D-Day, preliminary work began on the proposals that surfaced at Bretton Woods. The American effort was directed by Harry Dexter White, the son of Jewish immigrants from Lithuania and an unknown actor on the world financial stage when Morgenthau gave him the job of fashioning a reconstructed world economic order. His British counterpart was John Maynard Keynes, the world's pre-eminent authority on economics and international finance. Keynes had been a charter member of the twentieth-century British establishment and now, in the twilight of his long and distinguished career, was the elder statesman of the old order.

The relationship between these two men, whose backgrounds were so different, foreshadowed the ascendance of America as a world economic power after the war and presaged the end of Great Britain as a major international economic force. Roy Harrod, Keynes's sympathetic biographer, describes a 1943 meeting between Keynes and White:

White was difficult, there was no doubt; Keynes, although not sparing him in verbal debate, exercised tact and forbearance. White's own feelings were more subtle. Only a few years ago, before his star had risen, he had revered Keynes as the greatest living economist. Now he was confronting him as a negotiator on an equal footing—or rather, on an unequal footing, for he . . . represented the stronger power. . . .[3]

The people assembled at the conference represented a collection of keen intellects and bold visionaries. Henry Morgenthau, Jr., was one of the most influential treasury secretaries in American history because of his unique access to his longtime friend, President Roosevelt. He provided the conference delegates with an opportunity to see firsthand his fusion of New Deal financial populism and shrewd knowledge of international finance. He assembled a brilliant staff led by White. Dean Acheson, secretary of state under President Harry S. Truman, was a member of the delegation along with a host of names that would be important in the postwar governance of the world economy.

Other delegations were equally distinguished in personnel and creative in their thinking about the postwar international economy. Pierre Mendès-France, later to become prime minister of France, led the French delegation, whose members included the originators of the postwar European Economic Community. Delegation after delegation included individuals who would come to play an important role in the postwar world economy —either as the head of their central bank or as an important official with the World Bank or the International Monetary Fund.

The historical context of the Bretton Woods meetings did not escape the delegates. Meeting just three weeks after D-Day, during the first three weeks of July 1944, the participants could legitimately contemplate the existence of a postwar world in which the industrial democracies survived. The exercise, therefore, was given a concrete meaning and an urgency it could not have had earlier. While these meetings were under way, discussions surrounding the creation of the United Nations provided yet another impetus for the delegates to construct international economic institutions that would reduce political tensions and mitigate military conflicts.

Bretton Woods was seen as part of this process, and in fact it was officially called the United Nations Monetary and Financial Conference. There was an air of anticipation and hope, following years of despair, which penetrated the stuffy conference atmosphere usual in meetings of this sort. Even the typically gray demeanor of international bankers was unsettled by the significance of the meetings, the relaxed style of White, Morgenthau, and the other Americans, and by the majesty of the setting itself.

After being closed at the start of the war, the five-hundred-room Mount Washington Hotel, which housed the conference, had been refurbished at considerable cost in anticipation of a leisure-conscious postwar America. Its first guests were the delegates to the Bretton Woods conference. You can see today an advertisement for the Mount Washington hotel in the *New Yorker* magazine. Trading on the nostalgia for an era passed—

not an unlikely metaphor for the Bretton Woods system —the picture-postcard photo of the hotel is accompanied by a text that describes it as an "Edwardian resort which has flourished for more than eighty years." Guests "who desire the service and style of a bygone era" are invited to patronize this hotel, which sits in a "sea of evergreen, against the backdrop of the Presidential Range."[4]

The hotel was chosen as the site for the meetings, however, not only because of its size and availability. In an age when air-conditioning was not generally available, the July heat precluded many meeting venues. In a letter to White, Keynes viewed the prospect of being invited to Washington in July as an "unfriendly act."[5] Edward Bernstein, now a senior fellow at the Brookings Institution, revealed yet another reason for the choice of Mount Washington. "Morgenthau, even as Secretary of the Treasury, had had trouble getting into some of the fancy places . . . because he was Jewish," says Bernstein. "And he was determined that we wouldn't go to any place, where there ever was, at that time, any kind of distinction between Jews and non-Jews. . . ."[6]

For today's advocates of a "second" Bretton Woods to resolve current world economic problems, it is easy to become overly sentimental about Bretton Woods—the conference setting, the creative minds, and the visionary task. However, the specific circumstances of 1944, which encouraged the participants to reach agreement, are not present today. There was no world economy in July of 1944. The interwar years of economic nationalism effectively brought the world economy to a halt and the war was the nail in the coffin. "Much of the growth of trade," in the postwar world, says the economist Paul Streeten, "is a return to the pre-1914 situation which had been disrupted by the two world wars and a severe depression."[7]

The United States and Great Britain were essentially the only large industrial democracies extant in 1944, what with France and the rest of Europe (Sweden and Switzerland excepted) overrun by Germany. The Soviet Union was a participant in the Bretton Woods process but played a fringe role. Canada and Australia were relatively untouched by the war, but their economies were small. What today is called the Third World was, outside of Latin America, mostly a colonial appendage of a European power. Their role was minimal at Bretton Woods.

The Central Features of a World Economy

B EFORE proceeding further with the discussion of Bretton Woods, it will be helpful to have some general knowledge about how a world economy functions, independent of any specific institutional forms. Writings about the world economy have been enshrouded in an arcane language that produces an impenetrable barrier for the uninitiated that only permits practitioners access to the language of discourse. It need not and should not be this way, for a bit of background about the general character of a world economy is not beyond anyone's reach.

We start with a national economy closed to outside influences and then proceed to add other countries to the story. The national economy is more familiar to most of us because that is where we live and work. But the larger international economy is always buffeting us and affecting our economic fortunes, whether we are aware of it or not.

Some people organize the process of production and produce goods and services. In doing this, they employ other people and pay them a wage or salary for their services. The producer may rent facilities owned by others and be charged a rental fee that is another form of income creation—this time the income received by the owner of the property. Other sources of income are profits and dividends. These incomes form the basis for the purchase of commodities, and the act of buying a commodity produces a sale that enables the producer to go about his business.

If the sales are robust enough, profits high enough, and prospects for the future look good, the enterprising producer will consider an expansion of operations by means of a new investment. This is yet another stimulus to the economy via the income that is created by the producers of capital who hire people and pay them for their services. This process creates a neat little closed circuit, where income is created through production, and that income is used to purchase the commodities produced.

The story becomes a bit more complicated when the national economy is opened to influences from other countries. Some of the income might be used to buy things produced in other countries—imports—and some of the production might be sold abroad as exports. Imports represent income leakages out of the closed national circuit, because they are sales lost to producers from other countries and income that has escaped from the national economy. On the other hand, exports represent the obverse: an injection of income from abroad into the national economy. Every country would prefer to have more income injections into their national economy and to minimize the income leakages out of their economy.

Thus is born the mercantilist basis for intense economic competition among nations. It is logically impossible for every country in the world to export more than they import. Unless checked by some larger imperative, economic nationalism will generate an urge to create a favorable balance of trade through protectionist measures that could damage the fragile balance of cooperation in the world economy.

International trade, imports and exports among nations, is the backbone of an international economy. It need not be completely free and open. Countries may erect various forms of barriers to trade, such as tariffs or direct import restrictions, and they normally do restrict trade somewhat. Except for periods of war or the out-of-control economic nationalism of the 1930s, however, there is normally a functioning international economy that involves the movement of commodities through international trade with a greater or lesser degree of economic protectionism.

Now, a second complication has to be introduced into the story: money. So far, the economic parable has been told in terms of the movement of real, tangible goods and services. The idea of money lurked behind the story; now it must be brought front and center. Money is the lubricant that makes the gears of the economic engine work. In the closed-circuit economy confined to a national economy, money is needed to facilitate the process of exchange. If you worked for a firm and were paid in the form of the product you produced, you could take some of that product and barter it with someone else for the things you need. But the invention of money makes this exchange much simpler. You are paid in a universally recognized medium that everyone else is prepared to accept in exchange for their products. So the cumbersome process of bartering is replaced by the smooth process of money changing hands in exchange for goods and services. This is called the *transaction* function of money and is the first of several important uses of money.

Money is also used to denominate prices—its second, *price-signal*, function. When you earn a wage or salary and purchase another's output, you are in effect exchanging the fruits of each other's work. How much you can purchase depends upon prices; it defines how far your money will take you. The rate at which you exchange your hard-earned cash for commodities is identified by the price. These price signals, denominated in money, are critical in allowing information to be created and disseminated in the economy. The market is the place where the price signals are created in market economies. Buyers and sellers come together and conduct their transactions based on how the market, through prices, signals supply and demand.

Money also has a third function. You may opt not to spend all of your income and retain some of your money as savings for which you will receive additional income in the form of interest. Thus, money becomes a *reserve* to be retrieved and used at some future date when you have more need for it. Buying a house, sending your child to college, or simply saving for a rainy day are ways in which the reserve function of money is used.

The next complication takes us back into the world economy where money is added to the open real economy. Problems in the international economy arise because money is defined in nation-state terms while trade and their accompanying money transfers are conducted across national boundaries. When transactions occur involving any two countries, which nation's currency will be used? Or will a third country's currency be used that is not even a direct party to the transaction in international trade?

Consider what would happen if there were many currencies used in the United States, each issued by a state government. Every time you crossed a state boundary, a different currency would have to be used. What would happen if cars produced in Detroit were sold in California? Would Detroit's currency be used in the transaction or would California's; or would Mississippi's be used? This is precisely the complex problem that must be resolved in the international economy for it to function smoothly. Imagine how cumbersome and difficult travel across the United States would be if each day you crossed a border and had to change currencies. If you lived in some places in Europe, however, this would become second nature to you. Drive a day in many parts of Europe and you are in another country, fiddling with strange-looking pieces of paper and juggling difficult fractions in your head.

For the international economy to operate as an integrated world economy, the problem of whose money to use and how it will be controlled must be resolved. Money has to play an overarching integrating role to unite disparate countries that are driven toward competition by the need to run favorable international money balances—called the balance of payments. The centrifugal forces of competition outweigh any natural unifying forces. Money's job is to introduce some order into this potential chaos by providing for the reserve, transaction, and price-signal functions. As the seventeenth-century playwright Aphra Behn—considered to be the first Englishwoman to earn her living through writing—put it in one of her Restoration comedies: "Money speaks sense in a language all nations understand."[8] The designers of Bretton Woods pursued the objective of money-sense and attempted to create institutions that would resolve this most difficult of all international economic problems.

The Pre-eminent World Economic Power

T HE WORLD economy has historically grown faster when there is a pre-eminent economic power that writes the rules for the game, enforces their acceptance, and underwrites the risks. The United States did this during the Bretton Woods period, and Great Britain performed this function during Pax Britannica. This creates a perplexing paradox for twentieth-century liberals who are more comfortable with a world of greater economic parity and shared political power. Sustained periods of robust economic growth, however, are not associated with such conditions. Worldwide economic growth is historically more likely to occur when there is a pre-eminent economic power, prepared to structure the world economy to fit its own interests.

When political and economic power is more equally shared, economic nationalism becomes more intense. Countries have difficulty navigating through the narrow channel between acceptable economic nationalism and destructive protectionism. One country strays off course and others follow. The interwar period can be characterized this way, as can the late 1970s and early 1980s. The editors of the journal *Monthly Review*, Harry Magdoff and Paul Sweezy, point out that there were five currency and trading blocs, separated from each other, during the interwar period—the sterling, dollar, "gold," and yen blocs, plus a middle-European sphere dominated by Germany. "What is especially noteworthy about these blocs and the alliances formed among them," they say, "is that they pretty much prefigured the lineups of the belligerents in the Second World War."[9]

There is a contradiction, therefore, between shared

economic power in the world economy, which historically has produced lower rates of economic growth and
destructive economic nationalism, and a hegemonic
economic power that enforces an economic stability that
leads to economic growth, but at the cost of liberal values of equity. Hegemony cannot be sustained indefinitely, however, and during the period of pre-eminence
there is also a conflict over objectives in the world economy. To the pre-eminent economic power, "the apparent
indifference of others to these questions [international
economic stability] will often seem like the crassest nationalism and narrow-minded selfishness."[10] In a study
of America's changing role in the world economy, David
Calleo and Benjamin Rowland underscore this point:
"As the predominance of the superpowers recedes and
the world becomes more plural, nation-states are likely
to disport themselves in a new independence. Collective
international institutions which depend primarily on
hegemony will have trouble surviving once hegemony is
gone."[11]

The Bretton Woods Compromise

T HE FORMATION of the Bretton Woods system was
an amalgam of internationalism, on the one
hand, and a recognition that the United States
was the pre-eminent economic power, on the other,
whose mission was to structure a world economy after
the war that would avoid the errors of the Versailles
peace. Roosevelt in his welcoming message to the Bretton Woods delegates talked about this conference being
"one phase of the arrangements which must be made
between nations to ensure an orderly, harmonious

world," and Morgenthau was explicit about avoiding the "currency disorders . . . idle tools, wasted wealth [that] become the breeders of fascism and, finally, of war."[12]

The United States was entrusted with the primary responsibility for ordering the world economy and for seeing that basic tenets of internationalism were fulfilled. The two balls that had to be juggled—U.S. economic superiority and democratic internationalism—would have stretched the noblest of powers to its limits. The United States did an adequate job of balancing these two contradictory objectives, particularly in the face of the political divisions at home between xenophobic isolationism and idealistic internationalism.

America's rival for power after the war was Great Britain, but when the chips were down both sides knew where the power really was. Harry Dexter White in 1944, during discussions over the location of the IMF and the World Bank, said: "New York has become the financial center of the world. These British are just fighting uphill." Keynes, who wanted them located in London, reported back to his superiors: "I believe that we are on a losing wicket here." The *New York World-Telegram* in 1943 used another athletic metaphor: "The kid who owns the ball is usually captain and decides when and where the game will be played and who will be on the team. While international monetary stabilization is not baseball, it is a game." The editorial goes on to say that sharing power equally with the British "not only is not good baseball—it is not even cricket."[13]

The Pax Americana vision was the "American version of the Western liberal dream—a closely-knit world system of vigorously prosperous democracies, enjoying security from military aggression, permitting the free movement of goods, money, and enterprise among themselves, and promoting the rapid development and integration of those nations whom liberal progress had left behind."[14] For these objectives to be realized, however, implementing institutions and rules had to be devised. The most important involved international monetary relationships.

International Money

T HE PRE-EMINENT nation's currency must first be universally accepted in international transactions and become the *international currency*. If the international currency does its job well, it will not only be used for transactions, but it will also be held as reserves by the central banks of other countries against future unforeseen needs. The defining characteristic of the pre-eminent economy is that its national currency is also the international currency. The pre-eminent economy provides the wherewithal for its national currency to perform the reserve, transactions, and price-signal functions in its own economy and in the world economy.

Second, and separate from the question of which country's currency will become the international currency, is the rate at which one country's currency will be exchanged for another's. These *foreign exchange rates*, as they are called, are critical for commercial relationships in the world economy. Some mechanism must be found for establishing the price of one country's currency in terms of another's—either through international agreement, free markets, or imposition by the dominant power. In reality, all three mechanisms are used in different mixtures.

Certain obligations go with the pre-eminent economy's use of its currency as the international currency. It must be prepared to supply its currency to the rest of the world in the right amount to support the volume of world trade consistent with economic growth. The term used to describe this is *international liquidity.* Too much liquidity and the system tends toward inflationary instability; too little and growth is retarded.

The pre-eminent economy must stabilize the value of its currency at home and run low rates of inflation. Otherwise, the system loses its moorings and tends toward speculative instability, because the anchor currency no longer has a predictable value. The international-currency country must also have the political will to establish a set of rules and enforce them. When things go off track, and a country runs a persistent balance of payments deficit, the pre-eminent economy has to be prepared to underwrite the system's risks and become what the international economist Charles P. Kindelberger calls the "international lender of last resort."[15]

These monetary relationships in the world economy reflect an underlying political reality. "The design of a monetary system, underneath its technical drapery," say Calleo and Rowland about the monetary Pax Americana established at Bretton Woods, "naturally reflects the basic political pattern governing the overall relations of the member states," and Susan Strange reaches a similar conclusion about the monetary Pax Britannica of the nineteenth century: when countries "start to use . . . a currency . . . other than their own, . . . political consequences can be expected to follow . . ."[16]

3

THE POLITICS OF
INTERNATIONAL MONEY

COUNTRIES prefer not to concede dominance to
a pre-eminent economic power even though it
may be better for their own economic growth.
The parts are unable to envision their whole,
and economic nationalism is a far more powerful political force than any abstract rationality about the greatest
good for the greatest number. The questions are, how
does a country become *numero uno* and how does its
currency become the international currency? There is
no plebiscite, no meeting, no Gallup poll. It happens
because one country's trade position is so dominant
that every other country in the world seeks its currency,
to the exclusion of other currencies, in order to buy its
products. This was the condition of the world economy
at the end of World War II.

The United States was the only large industrial economy whose industry was still intact. In fact, it emerged
out of the war with a decidedly stronger industrial base

than it had when it entered the war, while every other industrial country saw its manufacturing capacity destroyed by the war. In Europe, there was an enormous need for capital for reconstruction, for consumer goods, for food, and so on. The European economies could not provide these items in the amounts needed, but the United States could. An American producer, however, would not want to be paid for his products in French francs or Dutch guilders. He wanted dollars. But how could the French or the Dutch acquire the dollars?

The United States took an enlightened position on this problem, compared with the actions taken after World War I, when the victorious powers cut off the defeated nations' access to the international currency, thereby setting the stage for the economic conflicts that contributed to the start of World War II. After World War I, Germany was forced to pay reparations in the hard currencies of the triumphant countries, when international cooperation dictated the opposite policy: the transfer of international currencies to the defeated powers so they could participate more actively in the international economic community.

John Maynard Keynes, as a member of the British delegation to Versailles, took sharp exception to the punitive terms of the peace treaty. His predictions about the consequences were eerily fulfilled. Writing in 1919, he said: "The existence of the great war debts is a menace to financial stability everywhere. . . . If we aim deliberately at the impoverishment of Central Europe, vengeance, I dare predict, will not limp."[1]

Keynes was determined at Bretton Woods to prevent a recurrence of the post–World War I economic chaos. This remarkable figure of the twentieth century bookends the two great peace conferences after the two World Wars. His influence on the reconstruction of the world economy after the second was profound. The leadership in the Roosevelt administration—led by Morgenthau and White—accepted Keynes's analysis of the mistakes of the Versailles Treaty, and they were prepared to avoid a replay of this sorry historical record. The problem was how the dollars could be exported to other countries. They could not simply be printed and dropped from an airplane. Economic mechanisms had to be created to permit an orderly movement of dollars in the world economy. This problem was resolved by a combination of the private worldwide market economy and by the institutions developed at Bretton Woods.

The Dollar as the International Currency

I N NORMAL times, the typical way in which a country acquires the currency of another is to sell it its products. But this option was generally not available immediately after the war; in fact, it did not become feasible until the middle to late 1950s. There was, first, no surplus of output in Europe to sell to the United States. Every little morsel of food or spare consumer good that could be produced in Europe was in such demand that exports were out of the question. Second, American products were generally cheaper and better in quality than were those produced in Europe. So the trade option was precluded for at least a decade as the way for other countries to obtain dollars. Other means had to be found.

Between 1946 and 1950, several mechanisms were devised to move dollars from the United States to Europe and Great Britain that reflected both the internationalism of Bretton Woods and the economic preeminence of the United States. One institution, created at Bretton Woods for this purpose, was the World Bank, whose actual name describes its functions precisely: the International Bank for Reconstruction and Development (IBRD). Keynes chaired the section of the Bretton Woods conference on the bank. The absence of such an institution after Versailles was central to his view of what went wrong after World War I and critical to what he wanted to see go right after World War II.

The role of the IBRD was to raise capital in the United States and Great Britain, primarily, and then use the dollars and pounds to make loans to the war-devastated countries of Europe for large capital reconstruction projects—roads, electric power, mass transit, and the like. Today, the World Bank makes loans only to the poorer countries in the world. This change in its orientation occurred around 1960; prior to that time, its lending attention was directed toward Europe.

In 1946, when the World Bank opened its doors in Washington, it was capitalized at $12 billion—a combination of capital subscriptions from its members and authorization to borrow. Only about $2¼ billion dollars was available, however, in 1946.[2] While not as large a bank as Keynes wanted, it was bigger than the American delegation preferred. The capital endowment was the foundation that enabled the IBRD to raise more money on Wall Street and in the City of London by issuing bonds and selling them to private institutions and individuals. It still does this today. The World Bank stands as a financial intermediary between the borrower and the individuals and institutions that are prepared to place their money in its care. It absorbs the risk associated with the investments of the country-borrowers. The Bank leverages its intial endowment into additional funds raised in private capital markets by providing a security curtain and the umbrella of confidence that tags along with any institution called *The World Bank.*

A large investor or bank was reluctant to lend money directly to European countries after the war in view of the bleak prospects for a rapid return on that investment. In addition, the scale of capital needs—tens of billions of dollars—was beyond the limits of the private capital markets. However, when the World Bank entered the picture to raise capital, it received a good response because of its name, its capital endowment, and the security underwritten by the full faith and credit of governments.

The export of capital through the World Bank quickly became inadequate to meet the large investment needs in Europe. More was needed, but it did not go through the World Bank, for the most part, after the onset of the Cold War. A narrow window of internationalism was quickly shut and the Bretton Woods institutions, that were never universally supported, lost favor.

The International Monetary Fund and the World Bank were not politically popular in the Congress in the 1940s, particularly among its xenophobic and isolationist members. On Wall Street, the financial community had also opposed the Bretton Woods institutions. This opposition from both quarters came out during the debate over ratification of the Bretton Woods agreements. During the Congressional debate, Frederick C. Smith of Ohio spoke for many of his colleagues when he opposed Bretton Woods "because I am an American, love my country, and refuse to surrender any part of it to foreign powers." His Senate colleague from Ohio, Robert Taft, was equally critical: "If we try to stabilize conditions with this fund it will be like pouring money down a rat hole."[3]

The opposition from Wall Street came from the banking community—the large banks and institutional investors who looked with considerable disdain at the Roosevelt administration. The American Bankers Association took a firm stand in opposition to the Bretton Woods agreements: "We . . . find provisions which, in our opinion, are financially unsound and, if adopted, might retard rather than promote enduring recovery." This sent Morgenthau and his troops into a state of apoplexy. They thought they had assuaged the banking community's concerns and the bankers would support, albeit reluctantly, the Bretton Woods agreements. Here is Morgenthau's answer to the American Bankers Association report: "Is it better for us to take the risk and spread it among forty-four partners, or to have five banks in New York dictate foreign exchange rates . . . and having London lead us around by the nose, which they have done in the last one hundred years."[4]

The *Christian Science Monitor,* in a February 1945 editorial, summed up the debate:

At the heart of the matter is the fact that this machinery would be put into the hands of public servants, paid executives of the governments involved, rather than in the group of private and powerful international bankers in "The City" in London, and in lower Manhattan in New York. You can see at once why there is a row involved. It depends on whether you think public servants can do the international job better than big private banks . . . who have been doing it in the past.[5]

This exchange took place in the mid-1940s. A few years later, the political climate was different: the New Deal was over, Roosevelt was gone, Morgenthau was no longer secretary of the treasury, and politics had tilted to the right. Taft and Smith were closer to the American political mood by the late 1940s. The State Department's plan for the reindustrialization of Germany had been given an urgency by the start of the Cold War, and the Morgenthau-White scheme for a deindustrialized Germany—the Carthaginian peace, as it was called—collected dust in library archives.[6]

With the start of the Cold War, the means for exporting capital to Europe took a bilateral twist. President Harry S. Truman inaugurated two large capital export programs—Point Four aid for Greece and Turkey and the Marshall Plan that kept the flow of dollars going from America to Europe to support their infrastructure reconstruction. Bilateral lending—no longer justified on internationalist grounds but on Cold War exigencies—was the second way in which dollars were shipped to the rest of the world, enabling the U.S. to fulfill one of the critical international currency functions: providing the rest of the world with dollar liquidity.

To the World Bank and bilateral loans was added a third mechanism for the movement of dollars overseas: military installations. Facilities were constructed and soldiers paid in dollars. These dollars were exchanged for local currencies and found their way into the central bank coffers where the military bases existed. In this way, dollars moved from the U.S. Treasury through the military to foreign central banks in support of international trade.

Yet a fourth mechanism for the acquisition of dollars by another country was through investments by American companies. Here is the origin of the modern multinational corporation. Some of this investment by American companies piggybacked on either World Bank or bilateral lending programs. The Marshall Plan administrators, for example, would develop a steel factory project in Belgium and invite participation by American companies. U.S. auto companies, which still have an enormous market in Europe, piggybacked on the Marshall Plan, as did retailers, producers of consumer goods, and virtually any other product one can think of. The normally circumspect U.S. Department of Commerce under President Ronald Reagan concedes this point: "Relatively large amounts of U.S. Government aid to the war-torn European economies (the Marshall Plan), much of it for rebuilding infrastructure, set the stage for large amounts of private U.S. direct investment in Europe."[7] The demand for dollars—an obsessive demand in the first years after the war—opened up vast opportunities for American corporate penetration that will never be replicated.

In today's world, it is difficult to imagine a proud nationalistic Europe and Great Britain willingly accepting the dollar invasion of their countries were it not for the terribly great needs they had after the war. A foreign army, an alien corporation, or another government affecting the economic planning process are not arrangements that are normally welcomed with open arms. But the late 1940s and early 1950s were unique times, and they produced uncharacteristic political behavior.

The Dollar and Foreign Exchange Rates

Y OU ARE about to land at Schiphol Airport in Amsterdam on your first trip outside of the United States. When the captain starts his descent and the cabin attendants commence their patter, your anticipation meter goes up a notch. The struggle with the luggage was not too bad and customs was much simpler than you had expected. Now you head for the *bureau de change*, carefully following the instructions received from veteran travelers. You approach the window and ask to change dollars into Dutch guilders. You have just become part of international finance by participating in your first foreign exchange transaction. If you visit more countries, you will quickly become aware of how important foreign exchange rates are for your travel budget.

Your head will turn almost reflexively to look at the little board in front of the ubiquitous *bureaux de change*. The important point to know about your tourist transactions is that everything you do in changing foreign currencies—finding the cost of meals in another currency, and watching the rates fluctuate—is *haute* international finance. Nothing done by the great international houses of finance is beyond what you have to do as a tourist. The principles are the same.

Did you ever wonder how these rates of exchange were determined? Since 1973, the rate of exchange of one currency for another has been permitted to "float"—find its value day to day and hour to hour in the free market, based on supply and demand. Starting in 1946, however, when the Bretton Woods agreements came into place, rates of exchange among currencies were fixed and not permitted to fluctuate very much, except in unusual circumstances that required international consultation.

The Bretton Woods agreements required every country to establish the value of its currency in terms of an ounce of gold. The United States, for example, set the value of the dollar at $35 to an ounce of gold. If every country established the value of its currency in terms of an ounce of gold, then there were rates of exchange among all currencies in the world. Say the German mark was set at 140 marks to an ounce of gold. The foreign exchange rate for the dollar against the mark would then be 4 marks to 1 dollar (divide 35 into 140). Gold was the common denominator, and one of its functions in the Bretton Woods system was to enable one currency to have a value in terms of all other currencies.

These rates of foreign exchange—the price of one currency vis-à-vis other currencies—were set by negotiation through the International Monetary Fund and were not permitted to vary beyond 1 percent. This was the

fixed part of the Bretton Woods foreign exchange system. If you were planning a trip in 1965 and calculating a budget, you would know with certainty how many marks your dollars could buy and you could plan accordingly.

The designers of Bretton Woods knew, however, that a degree of flexibility was needed. Economic conditions could change in a country and make defense of the fixed rate of foreign exchange untenable. In this way, the Bretton Woods system was a marriage—at times stormy —between stability and flexibility. The objective was to devise a stable system of foreign exchange rates that would pre-empt nationalistic, self-interest interventions by individual governments and at the same time provide the flexibility to respond to changing economic conditions.

Paralleling this official governmental part of the exchange rate system was the private market for the buying and selling of currencies. In these free foreign exchange markets, based in places like London, Zurich, and New York, rates of exchange fluctuated just like the movement of stock prices. The daily and hourly rates of exchange depended on the supply of and demand for currencies in the world, and these relative supplies and demands depended primarily on trade balances. Under the Bretton Woods agreements, each country agreed to stabilize its currency in the free market for foreign exchange within 1 percent in either direction of the official value that was established through the auspices of the IMF.

The IMF was Harry Dexter White's great achievement. Its task was to stabilize foreign exchange rates, within an agreed set of rules, in order to encourage the development of trade among nations. White's sharpest disagreements with Keynes were about the structure and functions of the IMF. Keynes envisioned a world central bank that would hold a country's accounts, permit borrowing through overdrafts up to a limit, and clear financial transactions among trading partners. Along with these functions, Keynes proposed a new international currency—the bancor—that would be used in international transactions and be largely independent of any one national currency. This would weaken the power of the dollar by submerging it into the bancor. The White plan was more modest, limiting the role of the IMF to exchange-rate stabilization and rejecting the other aspects of the Keynes plan, particularly the bancor idea. In so doing, he ensured that the dollar would reign supreme in the world economy, because there was no national currency that could compete with it for economic supremacy.

Stabilizing Foreign Exchange Rates

T HE CENTRAL bank of a country had the job of stabilizing the value of its currency on the free market within a 1 percent band. It did this by entering the market either by buying or selling currencies, depending on which was needed. If the value of its currency was falling below the 1 percent margin, this would signal the central bank that there was not sufficient demand for its currency in the free market. The central bank would take some of its dollars it held in reserve and buy its own currency, thereby increasing the demand for its currency. If the price rose more than 1 percent above the official IMF-established value, the central bank would simply reverse gears: it would sell some of its own currency in the free market. This would add to the supply of its currency in the private foreign exchange markets, take the pressure off the price of its currency, and drive it down to the acceptable range.

Fluctuations in the free foreign exchange market supposedly represented underlying economic realities between any two countries—primarily trade balances. Speculation, however, also played a role, as it does in any market of this sort. If the central bank could not stablize its currency within the 1 percent range in the free market, no matter how hard it tried, the country then had to take more drastic steps. Such incidents usually arose only on one side of the supply-demand equation, however. In general, it is much easier to stabilize the value of a currency when it is above the official value. All that is needed in this instance, when a currency is strong, is to create a larger supply and sell it in the market.

A persistently weak currency might require a visit by the country's central bank to the IMF if prior interventions did not bring the currency value back to an acceptable range. A series of escalating measures could be undertaken. First, the country in question might borrow dollars from the IMF to replenish its reserves in preparation for more aggressive intervention in the market. A war chest of dollars that could be used to increase the demand for the currency would be a signal to the markets that the central bank had the wherewithal to stabilize its currency. This confidence-building measure, by itself, could be enough to dampen speculative fires.

If this step was not sufficient, the IMF would look more closely at the underlying structural economic reasons for the continuing weakness of the currency and demand changes in the country's economy as a condition for the additional dollar loans. Here is the origin of the now-infamous IMF *conditionality* policy, which is applied to Third World countries today that have to borrow dollars in order to repay foreign debts.

If none of these measures successfully stabilized the value of the currency, then a final fail-safe measure was an official change in the foreign exchange rate. Through the auspices of the IMF, consultations would occur that culminated in a currency devaluation. If the German mark, for example, was weak at 4 marks to the dollar, fell below that rate in the free market, and could not be corrected by central bank intervention, it would have to be devalued and set at a rate, say, of 157.5 marks to an ounce of gold, or 4.5 marks to the dollar. The devaluation should encourage the purchase of German goods and discourage the sale of American goods in Germany, thereby correcting the underlying trade balance causes for the weak mark. Put differently, if you were in Amsterdam and heard about this devaluation, you should catch the first train to Germany, for now your dollars would buy 12.5 percent more in Germany than before.

The country whose currency was weak did not like being put through the Bretton Woods wringer. On this point, Keynes and White disagreed. Keynes envisioned an arrangement where the IMF would operate more like a bank and provide lines of credit that countries could draw on (up to a limit) without conditions. He also wanted the trade-surplus countries and the strong currencies to bear the burdens of adjustment along with the weak-currency deficit countries. White was troubled by what he thought would be an open-ended credit commitment by the United States, since realistically the dollar was the only currency that could underwrite the world's currency needs.

White's scheme for a limited-liability, dollar-based IMF prevailed because the Americans did not want to surrender the newly acquired economic pre-eminence of the dollar. "Now the advantage is ours here," said Morgenthau, and "I personally think we should take it," to which White added: "If the advantage was theirs, they would take it."[8] The Keynes bancor plan still has many adherents, and some variant of it inevitably crops up today during discussions of international monetary reform.

The flexibility built into the Bretton Woods monetary arrangements applied to all countries save one: the United States. The dollar as the international anchor-currency had to remain fixed; the $35-to-an-ounce-of-gold was sacrosanct and could not be changed without disrupting the entire fabric of the international monetary order. The reason for this goes back to the three functions of money: transaction, reserve, and price-signal. Central banks of other countries accumulated dollars for reserve and transaction purposes. If this key part of their portfolio was not stable and its value predictable, the reliance on the dollar would become shaky, causing a panic in the world monetary system. A manager of a central bank would not want to awake one morning and find that his portfolio of wealth was worth less than when he went to sleep. Like the keystone of an arch that holds up the entire edifice, the dollar had to remain solid, lest the system crumble.

The practical means of achieving the dollar's solidity was the pledge made by the United States to redeem any unwanted dollars for gold. Gold is an "archaic relic," Keynes once said, but it played a role in the Bretton Woods system up to 1971. A country could redeem its dollars for gold and use the gold as part of its reserves. In this way, gold was as good as the dollar and vice versa. Confidence in this arrangement was underscored by the vast supply of gold held by the U.S. at the end of World War II—about 70 percent of the world's mined gold. America supported this gold-exchange standard, as it came to be called, because of its virtual monopoly of the world's mined gold. The British preferred the Keynes bancor option that did not place such reliance on gold because, as the Bank of England said, the gold-exchange standard would amount to a "system where sterling will be less useful."[9]

The confidence-building feature of the arrangement worked much like your relationship with your bank. You maintain a checking account and expect to have cash made available to you on demand. If there is sufficient confidence in the arrangement, the actual act of redemption need not occur. You do not inquire at your bank every morning as to whether they have enough money to cover your account, except when rumors are rife about its not having enough money to cover all its liabilities. The same is true for the world banking system. So long as the U.S. had enough gold, was prepared to underwrite the system's stability by the pledge to redeem dollars for gold, and kept the gold-exchange price at $35 to the ounce, no one questioned the world economy's viability. For the first fifteen years or so, this arrangement, on balance, redounded to America's benefit; after that, it became burdensome.

The Political Economy of Bretton Woods

AMERICAN domestic economic conditions were significantly affected by the institutions established at Bretton Woods. Looking at precisely how the international and domestic economies intersected during this period provides a first instance of the critical importance of the international economy on U.S. domestic economic welfare. The first result of the Bretton Woods system was an economic bonanza for the United States. To be sure, there were difficult international monetary responsibilities placed on it that continued to cause political strains at home. In retrospect, however, most economic analysts would choose the economic results of Bretton Woods over its replacement in the 1970s. The key to the Bretton Woods windfall in the early period was the creation of dollar purchasing power abroad that enabled other countries to buy American goods and services. The economic circuit for the U.S. economy was, therefore, closed. Injections of export demand into the economy from abroad enabled the U.S. to run an economy with comparatively low rates of unemployment and with virtually no inflation.

During the first four years of Bretton Woods—1946 through 1949—the United States exported goods and services amounting to nearly $28 billion more than it imported from the rest of the world. This favorable balance of trade position—the excess of exports over imports—meant that dollar demand was being created in other countries that benefited the United States' economy. The decade from 1950 to 1959 produced another $30 billion in net exports. All told, the first fourteen years of Bretton Woods saw the United States exporting $58 billion worth of goods and services more than it imported from other countries.[10]

The injections from abroad, in the form of export demand, far exceeded the import leakages out of the economic circuit, and this was a fundamental factor in permitting the U.S. economy to have low rates of unemployment—an average of 4.4 percent per year during this period. It is difficult to pinpoint precisely the number of jobs that were attributable to these exports because many other factors affect job creation. My rough calculations put the number of jobs created by the Breton Woods–inspired exports at two million between 1946 and 1959, accounting for about one out of every five new jobs in the American economy during these years. This was accomplished with virtually no inflation. The average rate of inflation per year from 1946 to 1959 was only 1.7 percent.

The economic bonanza depended on American products being so superior in price and quality that the dollars exported abroad returned as purchases of U.S. products. "An ever-growing dollar deficit," say Calleo and Rowland, "created that ample liquidity which had, in turn, fueled the remarkable postwar growth of the world's economy."[11] The expansion of the American economy was largely the result of the uncontested competitive position it held after the war. But the Bretton Woods institutions made it all work better by facilitating the creation of the dollar liquidity in other countries that was used to buy U.S. products and employ American workers. The fixed-exchange-rate principle, adopted at Bretton Woods, provided the monetary stability that assisted the growth of world trade, and the dollar, as international currency, fulfilled its transaction and reserve functions.

On the inflation side of the economic ledger, Bretton Woods was a safety valve that permitted the escape of excess monetary steam from the U.S. economy. The monetary authorities could run a rather loose policy of monetary expansion with the confidence that any excess dollar creation could be moved abroad to satisfy an apparently insatiable demand for dollars in the rest of the world. The monetary circuit functioned smoothly, as did the production circuit on the real side of the economy, and the fine-tuning of an economy through the prudent use of monetary and fiscal policies raised the prospect of a future without economic hardship.

The Bretton Woods system redounded to our political benefit as well, because "America's monetary hegemony reflected a political relationship between Europe and America," writes David Calleo, who more than any other student of this period sees the critical importance of the economic arrangements in shaping a political order to our liking.[12] Other countries' obsession with acquiring dollars provided the United States with the political leverage that enabled its corporations to enter other countries, ushering in the era of the American multinational corporation. The United States was able to gain acquiescence to the introduction of its military into other countries where it had not been before—although there were certainly other considerations that encouraged this development. Nevertheless, as Calleo and Rowland point out, "In the postwar era, America's role in the monetary system and America's role in the military alliance have been two sides of the same imperial coin. Nuclear hegemony in NATO has matched dollar hegemony in the IMF. Dollars support troops, and troops support dollars."[13]

Bretton Woods politics in the world meant that other countries were reluctant to oppose American political positions—whether they were articulated in the United Nations, in NATO, or elsewhere—for fear of being cut off from the dollars. The political advantages of Bretton Woods for the U.S. followed on the economic windfall. Pax Americana was achieved with a dollar-enforced subtlety that required a minimal cost of direct intervention, when compared with the benefits received. David Calleo, once again, has captured the essence of the political economy of this period: "In the end, an international monetary regime . . . reflects an overall balance of political and economic power. A monetary system with special rules for one power reflects a group of states dominated by that one power. The system will last as long as the hegemony."[14]

White's Fate, Keynes's Fate, and the Dollar's Fate

I N 1943, Harry Dexter White prophesied that the dollar "will probably become the cornerstone of the postwar structure of stable currencies," because it is the "one great currency in whose strength there is universal confidence."[15] He was right about the fate of the dollar, in part, because of the institutions he designed for it at Bretton Woods. White's Bretton Woods scheme carved into stone the postwar economic reality: the pre-eminence of the United States' economy and the rule of the dollar. U.S. corporations became multinationalized and dominated commerce for more than two decades. The United States' political influence went largely unchallenged during the first fifteen years of Bretton Woods. The American military established over five thousand bases around the world. New York and the dollar replaced the City of London and sterling as the center for world banking and finance. Much of this would probably have happened after the war without a Bretton Woods. But Bretton Woods consolidated a Pax Americana with more subtlety and elegance because of White's contribution.

His role in the dollar's fate is part of the postwar historical record. White's own fate after the war, however, was not as glorious as that of the dollar. He was named by Whittaker Chambers—awarded the Presidential Medal of Freedom by President Ronald Reagan in 1984 —and Elizabeth Bentley as the highest-ranking government official who passed secrets through them to their Communist contacts during the war. White was passed over for the top job of managing director of the IMF by President Harry S. Truman, who had been given a 1946

FBI report on him, and instead he was named to the lesser post of U.S. executive director. This saddened White and baffled the Europeans who thought he was the obvious choice for the top position in the Fund.[16]

In 1948, White was called before the House Un-American Activities Committee, where his chief interrogator was Richard M. Nixon—a first-term congressman from California. Although White had the better of this confrontation, according to the newspaper reports of the hearings, he was not to have the opportunity to continue to defend his name. He suffered a fatal heart attack on the train after the hearings and died at his little farm in Fitzwilliam, New Hampshire, not far from the setting of his greatest achievement.

Several years later, President Dwight Eisenhower's attorney general, Herbert Brownell, released the internal security report given to Truman in 1946 on White, Alger Hiss, and others. Truman, as a private citizen, made a 1953 national radio broadcast in which he defended his decision to keep White in the government. By simply stating the charges against White and not commenting on their veracity, however, Truman let stand the accusations against him. To this day, Whittaker Chambers's believers see White as central to a wartime Communist conspiracy in the United States government, notwithstanding his role as the architect of the institutions of Pax Americana. This is an additional reason for conservative suspicions of the World Bank and IMF and explains why they have been reluctant to support them, for example, in the early days of the Reagan administration.

Keynes was in the twilight of his life when he took on the onerous task of representing Great Britain at Bretton Woods and in directing the bilateral negotiations over postwar loans for Great Britain from the United States. Physically frail throughout most of his life,

Keynes had suffered several heart attacks during the war, but that did not deter his transatlantic crossings, work in all-night drafting sessions, and his public utterances, which commanded a wide audience. At the formal dinner at the close of the Bretton Woods conference, the exhausted Keynes was a little late in arriving; "Tired, pale as a sheet, he was walking round the long table to his empty seat. Spontaneously everyone in the room stood up in complete silence while he made his way to his chair. It was an unspoken moving tribute to the master, the true prophet of this gathering."[17]

Keynes's reputation as one of the most influential thinkers of this century had already been acknowledged. The *General Theory*, written in the mid-1930s, gave him the dubious distinction of having a "revolution" proclaimed in his name. His writings on the Versailles Treaty influenced a generation of foreign secretaries and secretaries of state and taught them how to organize a peace. Keynes's ideas presented at Bretton Woods that were rejected by the Americans are perhaps as influential today as the ones he successfully introduced. In a real sense, the intellectual ghost of Keynes haunts today's discussions of international monetary reform.

Meeting in Savannah, Georgia, in March of 1946, the Bretton Woods countries ratified the principles adopted in 1944 through implementing legislation. Keynes, though frail and weakened, made the transatlantic crossing once again to lead the British delegation. Energized by the debate, Keynes rose to the occasion and delivered some of his most eloquent statements on how the peace should be organized. On the train ride back to Washington from Savannah, Keynes had a severe heart attack. He was able to make the journey back to England, but on Easter Sunday he died at his home in Tilton, Sussex.

PAX AMERICANA

ECONOMICA UNRAVELS

ᴀx Americana Economica began to unravel in the 1960s, not because of its failures, but because of its success. The United States could not come to terms with that success and tried to hang on to a system of rules that had been overtaken by history. A patch on one crack revealed another that required new emergency attention. Crisis management, instead of institutional reform, became a habit that the U.S. government has not broken.

Bretton Woods was like an old car that has seen better years. The problem is that it is hard to know when this point arrives, so instead of junking the car and starting over with a new one, the hope is that one more repair job will be the last for a while. It never is, and the time bought this way becomes increasingly expensive. Nevertheless, marginal calculations provide a rational veneer for the decision by showing how the short-term cost of repair is less than the perceived higher cost of replacement. There is also the uncertainty about how well the new car will run. For more than twenty years, the United States has been attending to the world economy as it would to an old car, justifying the piecemeal repair of the system by comparing it with the uncertainty of institutional overhaul.

The success of Bretton Woods carried with it an inevitable logic that ensured the end of Pax Americana Economica as it was practiced for the first fifteen years after World War II. For the system to function, the United States had to export dollar-liquidity to the rest of the world by running a persistent and growing balance of payments deficit. A large chunk of this was for the financing of European and Japanese reconstruction through private investments by American multinationals and public loans for infrastructure renewal. While the narrower trade balance was still favorable for the United States, the broader payments balance, which includes military assistance, foreign investment, and foreign aid, was negative. As the 1950s ended, the large negative payments balance from these three items could no longer be offset by the smaller positive trade balance.

"To have based America's future" argues David Calleo, "upon its episodic career as the dominant world power [was] a very bad bet historically."[1] Leveled by war, the European and Japanese economies could take advantage of American private and public capital-largesse to build modern factories with the newest technologies. It was only a matter of time, if the investments were used wisely, until the weak would overtake the strong—or at least achieve parity. This is much like professional sports arrangements—the National Football League, for example—which have a built-in mechanism for redistribution that makes it difficult for the best team to stay on top forever. In professional sports, it is the draft that provides for the redistribution by permitting the weakest team to choose first among the new players entering the league. In much the same way, Europe and Japan chose the newest and most advanced technologies when they rebuilt their factories, and the result was a "world with American power less overwhelming and American leadership no longer unquestioned."[2]

The approaching parity in trade relations produced repercussions in the dollar-based international monetary system, because the resilience of that system depended on the confidence the world placed in the dollar. This confidence was acquired in two ways: either by repatriation of the dollars held by foreign governments and banks through American exports or by their redemption for gold. Up to the end of the 1950s, America's competitive position in the world economy produced the large trade surpluses that enabled the United States to underwrite the Bretton Woods arrangements on the basis of the relative strength of its export position.

But this is precisely the paradox of Bretton Woods. The successful financing of European reconstruction by the United States made their products competitive with ours and reduced dollar repatriation via American exports. No longer did Europe need to import as much from the United States. In fact, they could begin to sell us some of their products that were becoming preferable to American-produced goods. When the repatriation of foreign-held dollars through the United States' trade surpluses diminished, the United States had to underwrite the Bretton Woods system by the sale of its relatively fixed gold stock. Gold's expansion, however, was constrained by the limited physical stock of gold in the world, and its production was controlled primarily by South Africa and the Soviet Union.

The Great Gold Rush of 1959–1961

G OLD—the rush to acquire it by Europeans and the need to hold on to it by the United States—signaled that there was a serious fracture in the Bretton Woods system. Toward the end of the 1950s, the dollars held by other countries exceeded their demand for U.S. products. "The American balance-of-payments deficit provided the world with the dollars it needed. But that cornucopia gradually came to be seen as a threat," said the *Economist* in a retrospective on Bretton Woods. "The more dollars that were held abroad, . . . the greater the risk that this 'overhang' might one day cause a run on the dollar."[3] The world economy had turned 180 degrees from its condition immediately after the war when Europeans were short of dollars and their demand for American products was insatiable. As the 1950s drew to a close, managers of dollar portfolios abroad caught the first whiff of a dollar glut.

The designers of Bretton Woods had provided a short-term remedy for this contingency: the gold fail-safe mechanism. If another country did not want to hold all their dollars, it could cash them in for gold, priced at $35 per ounce. The gold was as good as dollars and could be held as reserves by foreign central banks and converted into any other currency. The United States stood by its commitment to sell gold at the fixed price, and the world placed confidence in this fail-safe mechanism because America had nearly 70 percent of the world's mined gold after the war. As long as this objective reality persisted, any speculative panic that might occur could be quickly defused.

As the postwar European economic recovery gained

momentum, however, fissures began to appear in these arrangements. First, American exports became less attractive in price and quality and foreign imports came to be more attractive to American consumers. The competitive appeal of American products—the basis for the dollar-based Bretton Woods arrangements—could not survive indefinitely unless the U.S. had imposed an economic peace on Europe that left it permanently underdeveloped. But as we have seen, the idea behind Bretton Woods was precisely the opposite.

Second, the U.S. exported dollars at increasingly higher rates in the 1950s, when prudent financial management called for reversing gears. Administrative inertia prevented U.S. policy makers then, as it does now from seeing the critical turning points in the world economy when a shift in policy is needed. Bureaucracies tend to see things remaining as they are, because it is easier to follow the familiar policy path than it is to risk change.

Furthermore, once having tasted the fruits of Pax Americana Economica, the U.S. liked the flavor and it became addictive. Private multinationals did not want to reduce their overseas investment; in fact, they wanted to increase it. The U.S. government did not want to surrender its position of pre-eminence; in fact, we wanted to solidify it. This was revealed in the source of the dollar outflow from the United States, primarily of three types: foreign investment by multinational corporations, military expenditures, and foreign assistance by the U.S. government. This " 'imperial' deficit," supported the "costs of Pax Americana" and represented "official military or economic subventions or private capital investments to shape a new world economy."[4]

So at a time when a slowing down of the rate of dollar export was needed, the opposite was happening. At some point, this twin-edged sword—a slowing of the rate of increase in the desire to buy American products and a growth in the rate at which dollars were exported abroad—would come to plague the U.S. economy. The year 1958 was a watershed. In that year, for the first time, dollars held by foreigners exceeded the value of the U.S. gold stock in Fort Knox. This meant that the fail-safe mechanism of gold sales could no longer be justified. Coupled with this was the realization that dollar reserves in the world were greater than the demand for American products. All the ingredients were in place for a three-star financial panic.

In the next year, 1959, the U.S. had the second-poorest balance of payments recorded for any year after the war—indicating that the higher dollar outflows could not be supported by the repatriation of dollars back to the U.S. via sales of products abroad. Only the Korean War year of 1950 was worse. This reinforced the speculation that there were more dollars around than could be justified by America's export position. In sum, both the gold stock and U.S. export competitiveness were no longer strong enough to underwrite the world economy.

The confluence of these developments weakened foreign confidence in the viability of the dollar-based Bretton Woods system. In 1960, rumors began to circulate that the United States would have to change the dollar price of gold, which would mean that the dollar was being devalued, in order to restore the competitiveness of its exports. This scenario was one that everyone thought about but no one dared talk about, lest it happen. Every central banker has nightmares about holding on to a currency too long and seeing it devalued along with the wealth he is entrusted to manage. But a devaluation of the dollar would be far more serious because so much of the world's monetary reserves were in dollars. The devaluator's pen is mightier than any general's sword to a central banker.

To avoid being caught napping, the rational decision for any foreign holder of dollars would be to cash them in for gold while there was still enough gold in Fort Knox to go around and before the United States stopped redeeming dollars for gold—referred to as "closing the gold window." The larger global interest would dictate that everyone remain calm. But speculative panics in world finance do not work this way. Each person trying to protect a dollar-loaded portfolio wanted to cash in some dollars for gold. The attendant run on the dollar from each person's rational act would create the collective instability that everyone wanted to avoid.

The first of several speculative runs against the dollar in the next twenty years occurred with the great gold rush of 1959–61. In 1959 alone, the U.S. lost 10 percent of its gold stock. Starting from $23 billion worth of gold in 1950, the stock in Fort Knox had fallen by only $1 billion by 1955. However, between 1955 and 1960, the gold stock had declined by $4 billion to about $18 billion. In the decade of the 1950s, therefore, gold stocks had declined by nearly 22 percent.[5]

The arcane world of gold intruded into the 1960 presidential campaign when Senator John F. Kennedy pointed to the gold drain as one example of the campaign issue he raised against Vice President Richard M. Nixon about the decline in American prestige abroad. In October 1960, just a few weeks before the election, the free market price of gold reached a postwar peak of $40 per ounce, and this led to a flood of foreign-held dollars being cashed in for gold in the U.S. at $35 per ounce and then resold in the free market for $40—a profit of $5 per ounce made by playing the free market against the official market. At the time, Kennedy's use of the gold-rush issue appeared to be a bit gratuitous—the straws that politicians grasp at to win votes. In retrospect, however, there was more to it than that, since

Kennedy did try to restore America to its position of economic pre-eminence after he was elected. This campaign foreshadowed the one held twenty years later that swept Ronald Reagan into office on a similar pledge to restore American prestige, after successive runs on the Carter dollar in 1977 and 1979 drove the price of gold in August 1980 to over $800 per ounce.

The U.S.-European Dispute

K ENNEDY was elected in 1960 on the campaign slogan of "getting the American economy moving again." Translated into concrete policy objectives, this meant full employment. Kennedy's advisers knew they had to do something about the international economy, otherwise the full-employment goals would be more difficult to reach. If the U.S. expanded its economy, personal incomes would grow. That would mean more spending by consumers and businesses for everything, including imports from abroad, and this would make the international monetary system more unstable. The gold rush was a signal that the U.S. balance of trade was already too weak to support the dollar's international responsibilities and more spending abroad would only worsen the predicament. Kennedy's objective, therefore, was to find a way to expand the domestic economy without causing further disruptions in the Bretton Woods monetary arrangements.

The balance of payments "haunted all economic discussions," according to Arthur M. Schlesinger, Jr., an adviser in the Kennedy White House, and it was the one problem that Kennedy "felt least at home with."[6] Theodore Sorensen—one of Kennedy's closest and most trusted advisers—underscored this point:

The tools of deficit spending and easy credit were not so readily available to President Kennedy's fight on unemployment for economic as well as political reasons. The main reason was a problem of concern to few, comprehended by even fewer, and practically ignored by the party platforms and the popular press: the balance of payments. Yet few subjects occupied more of Kennedy's time in the White House or were the subject of more secret high-level meetings.[7]

Opinion was divided in the early 1960s on either side of the Atlantic about the cure for the international monetary crisis. The U.S. wanted to prop up the existing system by restoring America's trade position and reducing its dollar outflows. The Europeans, with the exception of France, were more interested in finding a new reserve currency of some sort to augment the dollar than they were in strengthening the American economy. France preferred a doubling of the price of gold, which would have sponged up the excess dollar liquidity at a faster clip and would have moved more gold out of U.S. hands into European control.

The United States tried to stop the growth in the rate of dollar outflow by pressuring Europe to open their economies to more American products through a reduction of European import barriers and by having Europe shoulder more of the burden of NATO military costs. From the U.S. point of view, these measures were justified as recompense for its postwar generosity. Coincidentally, they would also help Kennedy run a full-employment economy by creating jobs through exports, while holding the international monetary system at bay.

Europe, for its part, wanted to extricate itself from exclusive reliance upon the dollar, with its attendant dependence on the United States, by supplementing the dollar with some other unit of account in international trade. Their proposals would have moved the system more toward Keynes's idea of an international reserve currency that could be used for transactions but did not rely exclusively on the national currency of any one country. This proposal fit the political-economic circumstances of the world in the early 1960s as seen through a European prism. The Common Market was at its apogee; de Gaulle was in power and pursuing a nationalistic dream about the renewal of French glory at the expense of America's influence.

The two sides were far apart on the purposes of international monetary reform. National economic self-interest, always the prime motivator for foreign economic policy, played well to the respective political audiences on both sides of the Atlantic. The old shibboleth that foreign policy is not made for foreigners was certainly underscored by the economic disputes in the world after 1960. From Europe's point of view, the U.S. was asking them to solve its own economic problems. From the U.S. point of view, the Europeans were ungrateful for the economic support of their postwar economic renewal, which was the very reason why Bretton Woods was foundering. There is more than a kernel of truth to both of these propositions; it all depends on your vantage point.

Patching Up the System

T HE SEARCH for international monetary stability was pursued along two fronts: unilateral actions by the United States and the first collaborative new multilateral steps by the industrial democracies since Bretton Woods. The Kennedy administration tried to finesse the international financial problem by introducing measures that were designed to slow down the rate at which dollars were leaving the country. It did this, first, by an ingenious device called "operation twist." Rates of interest were increased on *short-term* financial investments for the purpose of discouraging the flow of dollars abroad from the United States and at the same time encouraging their repatriation from abroad back to the United States. The high rate of return that could be earned was, in effect, a bribe —more politely, an inducement—to keep dollars in the U.S., whose higher-interest-rate costs would be borne by the American people who borrowed money in these short-term capital markets. At the same time, in order to encourage capital investment for economic growth in the United States, the administration permitted *long-term* interest rates to remain low.

A second measure was called the Interest Equalization Tax, which imposed an extra tax on the borrowing conducted by foreign governments and corporations in U.S. capital markets and on the purchase of foreign stocks by U.S. citizens. This measure was designed to make it more costly for dollars to leave the United States by discouraging the access of foreign governments and companies to the dollars on Wall Street.

On the multilateral front, agreement on fundamentals could not be reached. The United States was unable to persuade Europe and Great Britain either to accept more of the financial burdens of NATO or to reduce import barriers. On the other hand, the U.S. would not agree to any change in the dollar-based world trading system. Instead, the industrial countries agreed on an expansion of the IMF's resources, on a means for stabilizing the free-market price of gold, and on a series of confidence-building gestures.

Chronologically, the first of the multilateral measures was the "Gold Pool" of October 1961. Each of the industrial countries contributed some gold to a fund, whose purpose was to create a buffer stock that could be used to stabilize the free-market price of gold. It was designed to dampen the sort of speculation that had occurred one year earlier when speculators exchanged their dollars for gold at the official price with the U.S. government, then turned around and sold the acquired gold for a higher price in the free markets in Europe. If the price of gold in the free market went above the official $35-per-ounce price, the managers of the buffer stock would sell some gold, which should reduce the free-market price.

Shortly after the Gold Pool was arranged, a second set of measures, called the Basel Agreement, was adopted. This was more a ritual of solidarity—not unimportant in dealing with financial panics—in which the heads of the central banks agreed to cooperate more closely in the stabilization of foreign exchange rates. Lastly, the capital subscriptions to the IMF were increased, providing it with an enlarged war chest to be employed against monetary instability. This represented a compromise between the European position that wanted to move the IMF toward Keynes's vision of a world central bank and the U.S., which wanted to hold on to the dollar-based world monetary system. With expanded resources, the United States hoped that the IMF would tiptoe toward playing more of the role of international lender-of-last-resort without actually becoming the world's banker, which was a position of power the United States did not want to relinquish.

While this overall strategy for dealing with the gold rush gave the U.S. a few years of breathing space, the international economic problems did not go away but continued to fester until they became a serious infection in the late 1960s. In her comprehensive history of this period, Susan Strange contends that American foreign economic policy was based on the belief that the 1960s would be much like the 1950s. "It was not foreseen," she argues, "that the United States for the first time might feel—and respond to—external pressures on its monetary policy-making."[8]

Unlike the earlier decade, however, which freed America from international constraints on domestic economic policy, the 1960s ushered in an era in which the intersection of international economic changes and domestic economic goals was far less favorable. The United States has not yet extricated itself from this dilemma; in fact, its ability to pursue high-employment and low-inflation objectives are today more sharply restricted by international considerations.

The legacy left by the Kennedy administration of dealing with international economic problems through crisis management is unfortunate. Managing crises is different from governing the world economy. Keynes's ideas for an international currency and a world central bank that exercises governance over the world economy had their advocates inside the administration—put forward with great force by the widely respected Robert Triffin—as they did in Europe. But these proposals were rejected by Kennedy in an effort to re-create the halcyon days of the 1950s-style Pax Americana Economica. An opportunity for reform of the system was missed during the early 1960s, when the present administrative style of handling world economic problems was established, an opportunity that has not been as available since.

It was a gamble, as Kennedy knew, to try fiscal stimulation at home while holding the world economy at bay. Arthur M. Schlesinger Jr., says that "Kennedy . . . used to tell his advisers that the two things which scared him were nuclear war and the payments deficit. Once he half-humorously derided the notion that nuclear weapons were essential to international prestige. 'What really matters,' he said, 'is the strength of the currency.' "[9] Kennedy's obsession with American power and prestige in the first two years of his administration blinded him to the possibilities of international economic reform that would share power and reduce the burdens on the American economy. It is not a coincidence that similar opportunities were missed with nuclear weapons. In both domains, he sought to reassert an American pre-eminence that history had decreed was no longer possible. Holding the fort on both of these positions continues to haunt presidents today as it did Kennedy. Sorensen reports this comment of Kennedy's to him: "I know everyone else thinks I worry about [the balance of payments] too much. But if there's ever a run on the bank, and I have to devalue the dollar or bring home our troops, as the British did, I'm the one who will take the heat. Besides it's a club that De Gaulle and all the others hang over my head. Any time there's a crisis or a quarrel, they can cash in all their dollars and where are we?"[10]

The Franco-American Gold War of 1967–68

E VERYONE knows that President Lyndon B. Johnson tried to fight a war on two fronts: against Communists in Viet Nam and against poverty at home. Fewer people are aware of yet a third front that was opened during his term of office—a gold war with France between 1967 and 1968 that eventually brought other countries into the fray.

The measures adopted by Kennedy, in conjunction

with the multilateral steps taken by the industrial countries, stabilized world money markets until about the middle of 1966. Johnson had pushed a bit further than Kennedy with direct controls on dollar outflows from the United States. For example, his administration asked American multinational corporations in February of 1965 to "voluntarily" restrain from expanding their foreign investment commitments. Johnson continued to place pressure on Europe—particularly West Germany—to absorb more military costs, with more success than Kennedy had. The one departure from Kennedy's approach was a willingness to entertain the possibility of a new international reserve unit that would free the world economy from its exclusive reliance on the dollar for international liquidity.

The breathing space acquired by the Johnson administration was not to last forever, and the Viet Nam War contributed to international monetary instability just as it overwhelmed Johnson's political base. Gold was once again the flash point. A second large run on gold occurred between 1967 and 1968 that undid all the patches that had been put on the system in the early 1960s. This time, the gold rush was driven not only by speculation in the world gold market; it was orchestrated by President Charles de Gaulle and the French government, as well.

French citizens do not trust governments and fiat—paper—money. They are goldbugs: hard-metalists who believe that the only real money is the kind that has the heft of gold or silver. Just as Americans have traditionally seen land as the great hedge against economic uncertainty and governmental capriciousness, the French hoard gold. Every French man and woman, it is said, has a little gold stashed away somewhere and for good reasons. Over the centuries, they have witnessed the collapse of many French governments who took the value of paper money with them when they fell. "Few Americans . . . fully appreciated," says Susan Strange, "how closely linked the long history of Europe had been with gold . . . while *assignats* and other currencies arbitrarily managed by governments had quickly been discredited."[11]

As the quintessential Frenchman, de Gaulle felt this in his bones. He knew his nationalistic attack on the gold-dollar link would resonate politically with his French constituency after France's humiliating military defeats in Indo-China and Algeria. And he also knew that gold was the Achilles' heel of America's worldwide influence—a cultural, political, economic, and military power he sought to undo for the greater glory of France.

In a long and rambling press conference on February 14, 1965, de Gaulle set forth his position on gold and the world economy. The general wanted a pure gold standard where all accounts would be settled in gold without the use of any national currency. Nor did he want to entrust this activity to an international monetary authority managing a dollar-backed bancor. He announced that henceforth France would convert any new accumulation of dollars immediately into gold. This accelerated the French conversion of dollars into gold that had begun in 1963, when the Banque de France had started to convert dollars at a rate of thirty tons of gold per month. One month before de Gaulle's press conference, the Banque de France added another $150 million to its previous rate of conversion.[12]

De Gaulle had effectively declared war on the dollar with his announcement that he would no longer hold dollars as reserves but cash them in for gold. Other private holders of dollar portfolios—banks and financial institutions—followed his lead because they did not want to be caught holding a currency that either would fall in value or become inconvertible if the United States closed its gold window and stopped trading gold for dollars. Johnson was forced to cash in some his political chips. He persuaded Harold Wilson, prime minister of Great Britain, to close the London gold market for a time when the rising price of gold in the free market threatened to add fuel to the speculative fire that was raging in world gold markets. He implored West Germany, Japan, and other allied countries to stay with their dollars and not contribute to the general's gold-conversion strategy.

Starting with about $18 billion of gold in 1960, America's stock went down by between one-half and one billion dollars each year, from 1960 through 1965. Between 1964 and 1965, however, the country lost nearly $1.5 billion when de Gaulle opened his war against the dollar. And by 1968, the U.S. gold stock dipped close to the important psychological barrier of $10 billion, which was considered to be the absolute minimum stock of gold needed to keep the dollar-based Bretton Woods system afloat.[13] By 1968, America's gold stock was half of what it had been in 1950.

The Viet Nam War and the Gold War

I N ORDER for de Gaulle's strategy to work against the dollar, he needed either a continuing flow of dollars into France or support from other countries. When the latter did not materialize in the mid-1960s, de Gaulle's strategy appeared to collapse, until the dollar outflows from Viet Nam War spending found their way into France and resupplied the general's arsenal.

In one of the more egregious ironies in a decade that was replete with them, the war in Viet Nam contributed to Johnson's vulnerability on the third-front gold war. France did not have an unlimited supply of dollars, and de Gaulle, being a military tactician, attempted a bold move: he tried a frontal assault in 1964 and 1965 by cashing in the dollars he held in the hope that others would follow his lead. The key was West Germany and Japan, but they stayed put. When de Gaulle ran low on dollars by 1966, the rate of depletion of the U.S. gold stock slowed somewhat, and the country had weathered the first assault.

De Gaulle's war against the dollar was given new life in 1967 by Johnson's escalation of the war in Viet Nam. Dollars left the United States for the war zone at a prodigious rate, only to find their way into the hands of Vietnamese businessmen and government officials, from whence they were moved to France, which was the traditional continental safe-haven for capital flight from Indo-China. It is impossible to know precisely how many dollars completed the circuit this way; some probably went to Switzerland and other traditional banking sanctuaries. The historic ties between France and Indo-China, however, led to the movement of a significant proportion of these dollars into French private banks and then into the coffers of the Banque de France.

The general had found a new source of ammunition in the war against the dollar. The dollars exported through Johnson's war in Viet Nam had now come full circle to the third front opened up by de Gaulle. Though not as troublesome as the war itself, the gold war was a problem the United States did not really need in view of the terrible political upheavals at home and the slowness of victory on the second front, the war against poverty.

Two towering politicians were eyeball to eyeball and

Johnson blinked first. On New Year's Day, 1968—just a few months before his announcement that he would not run for re-election—Johnson announced a series of restrictions on the outflow of dollars that involved virtually every aspect of the U.S. balance of payments deficit. All new foreign investment in Western Europe was to end, while investment in Great Britain, Australia, Canada, and Japan was cut to 65 percent of its 1965–66 levels. U.S. exports were to be promoted by special loan programs. Tourists were subject to foreign exchange controls and American banks were subject to further lending restrictions abroad. The foreign exchange costs of the military abroad were reduced by removing various dependents' allowances.

Measures, which at the time "looked remarkably draconian," in Susan Strange's words, turned out to be not as effective as Johnson had hoped.[14] And, in a curious way, they set the stage for the evolution of the world economy to a supranational economic order, as private U.S. banking interests found ways to evade Johnson's foreign exchange controls.

While Johnson was taking some unilateral steps to restore confidence in the dollar, his administration also pursued two multilateral technical solutions. In effect, the Gold Pool arrangement, which had provided for a buffer-stock stabilization fund, had been abandoned when France had opted out in June of 1967. It could no longer be sustained in the face of de Gaulle's war against the dollar. To replace the Gold Pool, the industrial countries—France excepted—adopted on March 17, 1968, what was called the "Two Tier Agreement." This provided a dual market for gold: the official one where gold sold at $35 per ounce and a free market where the price of gold would be permitted to fluctuate. This had always existed, but now the industrial countries were saying they would not intervene in the free market through the

Gold Pool to stabilize gold prices. The Two-Tier Agreement set the stage for the total collapse of the gold-dollar link that was to occur in the summer of 1971.

The second technical approach to this wave of international monetary instability was the creation of a new reserve unit—called the Special Drawing Right (SDR)—at a conference in Rio de Janeiro in 1967. Long on the table for discussion, the crisis of 1967–68 forced the United States to drop its objections to a new international reserve unit, and it accelerated the move toward the creation of SDRs, which were credits that could be drawn on by member nations through the IMF. Backed initially by the dollar and since 1974 by a basket of currencies and gold, SDRs moved cautiously toward Keynes's bancor idea: an international reserve unit that could be used in international trade that was not dependent on any one country's national currency.

In March of 1968—almost simultaneous with Johnson's surprise announcement of his withdrawal from the presidential campaign—the industrial nations meeting in Stockholm inaugurated the SDR system. By providing for the conversion of dollars into SDRs instead of gold, some heat was taken off the gold markets, particularly in official central bank transactions. The United States convinced European and Japanese central bank managers—again with the exception of France —to convert dollars into SDRs instead of gold and this bought a few more years of breathing space. At the same time, the events of May 1968 in France undid de Gaulle's power, and his successors did not have the will to prosecute his gold war with the same fundamentalist zeal.

Johnson, in his memoirs, characterized his policy toward de Gaulle as one of "polite restraint" during the height of the gold war in 1967 and describes, with uncharacteristic irony, how he tried to help him during the May 1968 upheaval in France:

Events caused a deterioraton in France's trade balance and a flight from the franc. De Gaulle and his government had been most uncooperative in the previous monetary difficulties. Nonetheless, in July we led the way with other nations in arranging a $1.3 billion stand-by credit for France. The international monetary system is not a field for pettiness or retribution.[15]

The two great protagonists in the gold war left the world political stage at about the same time and gave way to new actors. It was left to President Richard M. Nixon to bring to a close both the war in Indo-China and the gold war.

Nixon's Gambit

B Y THE start of the 1970s, "the affluent alliance had come to an end of the road, the bottom of the barrel of palliatives and easements," observes Susan Strange. "By 1971 the disorder was getting too serious for aspirins."[16] Johnson's patches on the system were the last. All that remained was for President Richard M. Nixon to compose the requiem. This is the same Nixon who had squared off against Harry Dexter White, the architect of Bretton Woods, at the House Un-American Activities Committee in 1948 over Communist infiltration of the American government during the war. Now he was ending what White had begun, but for reasons far different from those of Nixon's earlier knee-jerk anticommunism. For all of his reputation as a devious politician, it is fair to say that by 1971 Nixon had few options other than to end the Bretton Woods arrangements as White had conceived them.

The dollar crisis of the late 1960s was a replay of all

the crises that had occurred earlier in the decade. Some pressure was taken off America's gold stock by the fall of de Gaulle, the two-tier gold-pricing arrangement worked out during the Johnson administration, the SDRs, and the emergence of the German mark as a currency unit that was increasingly used in European trade. This last development added a new subplot. By the late 1960s, the West German economy was booming. It was accumulating trade and financial surpluses and beginning to play a more active role in European political and economic affairs.

Europe groped for a new way to organize its monetary affairs in the face of the dollar's instability and American unwillingness to take the steps that Europe saw as necessary to stabilize the dollar. Couple this with their opposition to the war in Indo-China and disagreements over policy toward the Soviet Union, and all the conditions were present for an attempt to break away from dollar dependency. The mark became a logical alternative.

On the other side of the Atlantic, the American society looked increasingly unstable and the dollar less of a safe haven. Amplified by the political opposition to the war in Indo-China and an apparent inability of the government to bring the war to a close, the United States looked wobbly from several thousand miles away. On the monetary front, dollars continued to flow out of the United States but with one difference: by the start of the decade, it reached flood stage. In 1970, nearly $11 billion left the United States, followed by $30 billion in 1971.[17] This compares with a peak in the previous decade of $3.4 billion in 1960 and again in 1968.

The same old problem existed: too many dollars floating around the world without a home. Neither the U.S. trade position nor its gold stock was adequate to the task of providing a nesting place for these dollars. From the standpoint of the Europeans, this was a time bomb that threatened to go off in their collective faces, since they were the ones holding the bomb while the United States controlled the fuse. If Europe began cashing in the dollars for gold, the bomb could go off. So, instead, dollars were moved into other currencies—primarily Swiss francs and German marks. During one four-day period in 1971, $3.7 billion was moved out of dollars into other European currencies.

Something had to give. The system had been stretched like a rubber band until it was about to snap. Nixon sent his recently appointed treasury secretary, John Connally, to Europe in the spring of 1971 to persuade the allies to give the dollar a little more breathing space. Henry Kissinger describes him as "the most formidable personality in the Cabinet," and "Connally's swaggering self-assurance was Nixon's Walter Mitty image of himself."[18] Connally's style was, to put it mildly, blunt. Accustomed to circumspect and neutral language, the central bankers of Europe were not prepared for the Texas-style tongue-lashing meted out by Connally. Perhaps if the TV show "Dallas" had been on the air at that time, they would have understood Connally better. Such tough talk, in any event, was misplaced in view of the political-economic power relations in the world in 1971.

The message from Connally was one heard many times before. Europe should take on more of the NATO defense costs, markets should be made more accessible to American exports, and Europe should cooperate more closely in dollar-stabilization strategies. And the answer was also predictable, having been heard before: the U.S. should accede to international arrangements that would reduce the role of the dollar in the world economy; it should end the war in Indo-China, which would stop a large part of the new dollar outflows. Added to this was a new demand that the United States should be more willing to enter into a dialogue with the Soviet Union— détente—in order to open up new markets for American and European exports.

When Connally returned and briefed Nixon on his European conversations—no doubt filtered through his own biases—an internal deliberative process that had been going on inside the administration was given added urgency. A working committee led by Paul Volcker, under secretary of the treasury for monetary affairs, had been developing options in case an international monetary emergency should occur. He was a key actor in the decisions that led to Nixon's August 1971 speech.

Volcker's career is based on detailed knowledge of how the U.S. Treasury works and how the private banking system operates. After graduate studies at Harvard and the London School of Economics, he took a staff position at the New York Federal Reserve. In 1957, he left the New York Fed and joined Chase Manhattan bank. Volcker worked on international monetary affairs in the Kennedy administration as head of the Office of Financial Affairs from 1962 until 1965, when he rejoined Chase Manhattan. Nixon called him back to the Treasury in 1969 to become under secretary for monetary affairs from 1969 to 1974, which was the position that put him in charge of fashioning policy options for the Nixon administration. After a year's "halfway house" at Princeton University, Volcker became president of the New York Federal Reserve. President Jimmy Carter plucked him from this second-most-powerful position in the Federal Reserve system to become chairman of the Federal Reserve Board in the summer of 1979.[19]

Volcker is one of those public figures whose enormous power and influence was behind the scenes until recently, when his name has become well known. The

Washington Post gossip columnist reported about a hockey game at the Capital Centre attended by various dignitaries—Vice President George Bush and his wife, the Canadian ambassador and his wife, Supreme Court Justice Sandra Day O'Connor and her husband, and Paul Volcker, among others. "The evening went well and the hockey fans applauded politely as the celebrities were introduced, except when Volcker's name came up —then the fans booed."[20]

Joanne Gowa, who has written about the events surrounding Nixon's 1971 speech, obtained a copy of Volcker's June 1969 report to Nixon through the Freedom of Information Act. The report says the "basic aim" of international monetary reform is to "free . . . foreign policy from constraints imposed by weaknesses in the financial system." The independent Federal Reserve Board, under its chairman, Arthur Burns, echoed this sentiment: "It is one of the proximate objectives of United States balance of payments policy . . . to be able to carry out government overseas operations at levels determined entirely . . . by the extent to which they are thought to promote basic United States objectives such as international peace and security."[21] Europe's fears that all the U.S. wanted to do was prop up the dollar were justified, and the Nixon administration, like its predecessors, continued to be blind to the fact that: "The slow transition from American hegemony to a more plural world order is not, in itself, a defeat for American policy. On the contrary, it is precisely the outcome that might have been expected to follow from the policy itself."[22]

But this enlightened view was clearly one that neither Connally nor Nixon could entertain. It would have taken a massive effort to turn around an American international economic policy that had been in place for a quarter century. International monetary policy, however, was a much lower order of priority for Nixon, who was besieged by political protests at home and a war abroad. Nixon's interest in these matters is at best characterized as keeping them at bay so he could pursue his international political objectives and at worst by his comment on the Watergate tapes that he did not "give a (expletive deleted) about the [Italian] lira."[23] As Nixon contemplated the coming presidential campaign, he no doubt recalled the role that the 1960 gold rush played in his defeat by Kennedy—a defeat that had left a searing impression on him—and he wanted to avoid a replay of that campaign.

So the stage was set for the high drama of August 15, 1971. In the first few days of that month, America's gold stock fell below the important $10 billion psychological barrier for the first time. Following a weekend meeting at Camp David, Nixon appeared on television and announced his New Economic Policy. He became the first president to use wage and price controls in peacetime; he reduced taxes and domestic government expenditures and announced a series of measures designed to increase employment and reduce inflation in preparation for his 1972 election campaign. It was his international economic pronouncements that were most far-reaching, however. He closed the gold window by suspending the convertibility of dollars into gold, and he imposed a 10 percent surcharge on all imports to restore some balance to U.S. international monetary flows. "With one dramatic gesture," says Henry Kissinger, "Nixon had broken the link between the dollar and gold, thereby opening the way for effective devaluation. . . . The industrial democracies, especially Japan, were in a state of shock . . . it was seen by many as a declaration of economic war on the other industrial democracies. . . . "[24]

By far the most important measure was his closing of

the gold window. "By suspending dollar convertibility unilaterally," writes Susan Strange, Nixon "obliged other governments either to accumulate and hold non-convertible dollars; or to sell them for whatever they would fetch on a free market, thus effectively revaluing their currencies."[25] It was an astute move. The dollar had nowhere to go but down when it floated, because it had been overvalued for years. This made the dollar cheaper in the world and American exports cheaper as well. The ball was now in Europe's and Japan's court; Nixon and Connally could sit back and watch over the net for a while. About a month later, Connally went back to Europe to address the monetary managers from Europe and Japan. "We had a problem," he said, "and we're sharing it with the world—just like we shared our prosperity. That's what friends are for."[26]

The dollar's effective devaluation was confirmed by the Smithsonian Agreement of December 1971, when a deal was struck: the United States would drop the 10 percent surcharge on imports in exchange for a revaluation of European and Japanese currencies. This meant a devaluation of the dollar against European currencies of about 10 percent on average and 17 percent against the Japanese yen. The industrial countries still hoped to maintain the system of relatively fixed exchange rates, but they did acknowledge how difficult this would be by widening the acceptable band of free-market fluctuation in exchange rates from the previous 1 percent to 2.25 percent.

"A truce not a peace settlement" is the way Susan Strange characterizes the Smithsonian Agreement.[27] The effort to hold on to one last vestige of Bretton Woods —fixed exchange rates—did not survive and "by March, 1973," according to the *Economist*, "all the major currencies had stopped fixing their currencies in the dollar band. Floating had begun."[28] What had sealed the coffin of fixed exchange rates were the continuing problems caused by an excess of dollars in the world—about 90 to 100 billions of Eurodollars—and the emergence of a new actor, now playing a principal role, who heretofore had a bit part in the international financial drama. That new actor was OPEC. In response to the dollar's devaluation, oil companies raised crude oil prices from around $1.25 a barrel to a little over $3 per barrel. While not engineered directly by OPEC, the increase in oil prices by the major companies paved the way for OPEC's assault on the world economy in the fall of 1973.

Eulogies now seemed appropriate both for the dollar and for Bretton Woods. "The old order, that, through the later 1960s, had alternatively crumbled and given way and been patched up and underpinned, was gone now."[29]

The Dollar's Reprieve

THE REPORT of the dollar's death was an exaggeration. In one of those curious ironies of international monetary affairs, OPEC commuted the dollar's death sentence. In the fall and winter of 1973, OPEC increased oil prices fourfold to a little over $12 per barrel. However, the oil-producing countries, notwithstanding their hostility toward the United States, stayed with their practice of accepting only dollars for payment —not yen, not marks, not gold, only dollars.

The dollar had been given a reprieve. It was 1950 all over again, because the oil-importing countries of the world desperately needed dollars to continue buying the same volume of oil but with more dollars because of the higher price. The United States was in the driver's seat once more, behind the wheel of a new auto after junking the old one in 1971. With the country's political-economic influence restored, it could for a while once again run a domestic economic policy without having to cast too many glances over its shoulder.

In the 1950s, the United States had considerable freedom for maneuver in domestic economic policy because all the world's economic forces reinforced its national economic objectives. This was reversed in the 1960s after Europe achieved trading parity, and the United States held on too long to the role of the dollar in international political-economic affairs. The coming together of these developments in the events of 1971–1973 portended the sort of economic realignment that should have led to new international systems of financial governance. But all this was upset by OPEC. The dollar once again was king, but the U.S. economy was not really strong enough to support its reign.

Susan Strange has summarized the lessons of the period from 1950 through 1973 this way:

National governments and central banks were apt to react to crisis situations arising in the gold and foreign exchange markets rather promptly . . . the same governments when faced with a perceived need to adapt or modify established international organizations, or to construct new ones, were apt to be much slower in their responses, more suspicious of each other's motives, and more jealously defensive of their perceived national interests.[30]

The sluggish response by governments to the monetary upheavals of the 1970s has left the world with an international financial baggage that weighs down economies with a rigid monetary austerity and has contributed to the slow-growth, high-unemployment 1980s.

II

The

Supranational

Economy

5

SUPRANATIONAL MONEY

FOR EVERY dollar in a bank or savings and loan association inside the United States, there is another 50 cents held in banks outside of the country that are beyond the regulatory reach of the banking safeguards we take for granted. This mystery money is called Eurodollars—dollar deposits in both U.S. and foreign banks in other countries. They cannot be held or crumpled and, says Richard F. Janssen of the *Wall Street Journal*, have "some things in common with an atom. You can't see one. The concept boggles the mind. And experts are deeply concerned over how best to harness its power."[1]

Because the dollars are not technically considered inside the United States, they escape regulation and protection by the United States government. Neither the Federal Reserve Board, the comptroller of the currency, nor the Treasury Department look after the safety of these dollar deposits as they do for bank accounts inside the United States. Unlike a checking account, the Federal Deposit Insurance Corporation does not insure Eurodollar deposits. The American government does not even have its own count of the size of Eurodollars because, according to the distinguished international economist Fritz Machlup, "as 'stateless money' they escape national enumeration by the monetary census takers."[2]

Eurodollars represent the first truly supranational form of money. Their growth and evolution is completely in the hands of the private banking system and answer to no government or public authority—whether national or international. They are "of this planet," said the economist, Lord Nicholas Kaldor, in a 1980 speech in the House of Lords, "but . . . not really under any country's rules or jurisdiction."[3] Although answerable to no public regulatory authority, expatriate Eurodollars and their movement through supranational banks have a profound impact on domestic monetary policy and on economic welfare. Private supranational banks need pay scant regard to governments, but governments cannot ignore the machinations of stateless Eurodollars, which have contributed to economic austerity and financial instability in the 1980s.

In 1984, there were over 1 trillion Eurodollars in the world economy which support international trade and form a significant part of world monetary reserves. Until the mid-1980s, when their rate of growth slowed somewhat, Eurodollars had been growing at an average annual rate of about 25 percent after the deregulation of international money between 1971 and 1973, compared with only a 4 percent rate of growth in the volume of world trade.[4] Spurred on by the revolution in information processing and communications, what Kaldor calls this "uncontrolled international credit creation in the world market" circles the globe in a matter of seconds and roosts wherever the short-run returns are high enough and the risks are acceptable. "The world of stateless money," writes the normally circumspect *Business Week*, "has in turn bred a stateless banking system in which national boundaries mean very little. . . . Now international commerce is totally dependent on this new supranational banking system."[5]

In the past decade, this supranational currency has become a dominant force in international financial markets, in worldwide banking, and in the lending activities of U.S. supranational banks. Shrouded in arcane banking jargon, the Eurodollar market, says the Joint Economic Committee of the U.S. Congress, "is perhaps best understood only by the practitioners employed by banks and other financial institutions. . . . To the uninitiated, the Eurodollar market seems to be a financial black box into which goes American money and from which comes credit for foreigners."[6] But it is not only the "uninitiated" who are befuddled by the Eurodollar system. "Like the sorcerer's apprentice," writes James Gipson, the head of Pacific Financial Research, a Beverly Hills, California, investment counseling firm, "the world's central bankers watch the explosive growth of the paper economy without being able to stop it."[7]

In 1976, the Congressional House Committee on Banking, Currency, and Housing conducted a comprehensive study of the banking system and published their findings in a series of reports under the title *Financial Institutions and the Nation's Economy*, known as the FINE studies. The volume on international banking expressed bewilderment about how the growth of the Eurodollar system could escape regulatory scrutiny. Its "growth has been encouraged by the absence of regulatory restraints," the study said, and "perpetuated by bank regulators who know too little about it to be able to determine whether and what form of regulation will be beneficial."[8] What is more perplexing is how the com-mittee's 1976 warning went unheeded: "It does seem remarkable that a narrow sector of the private banking system has been permitted or encouraged to assume quasi-governmental functions and that so much control over a financial market which is so important to so many nations has been concentrated in so few hands."[9]

How It All Began and How It Works

T HE ORIGINS of Eurodollars in the early 1950s are caught up in the start of the Cold War. "It is the Soviet Union that gets credit for accidentally fa-thering . . . the biggest and most efficient form of capi-talist finance," says Richard F. Janssen of the *Wall Street Journal*.[10] After the Chinese Revolution in 1949, the United States took steps to freeze Chinese accounts in American banks. To evade this move, the Chinese moved their dollar accounts into a Russian-owned bank in Paris, the Banque Commerciale pour l'Europe du Nord. The cable address, writes Anthony Sampson, hap-pened to be "Eurobank"—hence the origin of the term "Eurobanking" to go along with "Eurodollars."[11] Not all Chinese accounts escaped the American freeze, how-ever; when President Richard M. Nixon reopened dis-cussions of normal diplomatic relations with China, this issue became one of the more difficult ones to resolve.

Seeing what happened to the Chinese accounts in American banks, and "in the midst of the Cold War," says Dennis Weatherstone, chairman of Morgan Guar-anty Trust Company, "the Russians obviously preferred to deposit their dollar holdings somewhere other than in the U.S."[12] So as the Cold War shifted into high gear, Russia moved its dollars into a branch of their own bank in the City of London: the Moscow Narodny Bank. At that time, the City of London was a self-governing financial enclave that provided both banking secrecy and protection from any outside incursions that would threaten the viability of bank accounts. This "financial Samarkand," as Susan Strange describes it, was a "market place for the financial dealings of the world," and its new financial toy—Eurodollars—became the "great technological break-through of international finance in the mid-twentieth century."[13]

In the 1950s, activity in the Eurodollar system was minimal. "Soviet secretiveness, and the relatively minor amounts involved, kept these pioneering Eurodollars from making much of a splash," writes the *Wall Street Journal* reporter Richard F. Janssen. "However, they proved the feasibility of keeping a currency in a bank outside its country of origin, a precedent OPEC would follow two decades later. . . ."[14]

With the Bretton Woods system functioning smoothly in the 1950s, any dollars that were held in foreign accounts quickly made their way into the transactions stream of international trade. Few were idle, as Europe needed all the dollars it could find to pay for the American products it wanted to buy. Toward the end of the 1950s, however, Eurodollar growth began to exceed the demand for U.S. products. This development led to the start of a Eurodollar lending market. In 1957, the first large Eurobond issue occurred, a new issue of bonds for a Belgian oil company, Petrofina, worth $5 million and bought with Eurodollars. This new wrinkle in the Eurodollar system—the floating of bond issues— was to play a critical role in world finance after 1960, when the Eurodollar system began to mature.

The Eurodollar system works much like the domestic

banking system in which you participate. You deposit money in a checking or savings account and the bank turns around and lends out a portion of your money. They pay you interest (initially only for savings accounts, but now for some checking account as well) on your deposits and lend out your money at a higher interest charge so they can cover their operating costs, interest payments to you, and make a profit.

The Eurodollar system works much the same, but with a few differences. The accounts are in dollars but held in banks outside of the United States, in both American and foreign banks. Deposits are for large amounts, and the Eurodollar system is called a "wholesale" banking market because it deals only in large chunks of money on both deposit and loan transactions. It is more like a savings account than a checking account in that Eurodollar accounts earn interest. A depositor participates in a Eurodollar account by purchasing a certificate of deposit for a fixed sum that must be held for a specified time period in order to earn the full amount of interest. Today, there is a comparable financial instrument in the United States that can be purchased at a savings and loan association or at a commercial bank for a smaller amount of money. A certificate of deposit is bought for a specific sum above some minimum, and the purchaser cannot gain access to the money, without a penalty, until it matures. This is the way a Eurodollar account works.

The Eurodollar system needed time to ripen before it blossomed into what *Business Week* characterized as a "vast, integrated global money and capital system, almost totally outside all government regulation, that can send billions of . . . 'stateless' currencies hurtling around the world 24 hours a day."[15] Neither the deposits nor the loans were of a size that would warrant this description in the 1950s, nor was the communications system then adequate to the task of a worldwide capital market.

Two developments in the 1960s placed the Eurodollar system on a trajectory toward the *Business Week* description: the beginning dollar saturation in Europe that idled some dollars in banks and the accompanying regulation of investment-dollar outflows from the United States. Prior to these developments, the Eurodollar arrangements were known by few and understood by even fewer—except, perhaps, for Russia and its East European bloc, who needed a sanctuary for their dollars. Paul Einzig, one of the most dogged investigators of the Eurodollar system, explains how he initially came into contact with it: "The Eurodollar market was for years hidden from economists and other readers of the financial Press by a remarkable conspiracy of silence. . . . I stumbled on its existence by sheer accident in October 1959, . . . and when I embarked on an enquiry about it in London banking circles several bankers emphatically asked me not to write about the new practice. . . ."[16]

The Cat and Mouse Chase Between the Regulators and the Regulated

T HE GREAT surge in Eurodollar deposits and loans in the 1960s occurred in response to the U.S. government's efforts to control private capital outflows. American multinationals were investing in Europe and other places, and the dollars that left the United States this way were one of the important sources of the U.S. balance of payments deficits. When American exports lost some of their attractiveness—as we saw in the previous chapter—the dollars could not be repatriated through sales of U.S. products but were cashed in for gold. As regulations were placed on these private capital leakages, the Eurodollar markets responded by plugging the leaks. "Of all the forces responsible for the creation and expansion of the free Euromarkets and the pool of stateless money," says *Business Week*, "none has been as powerful as the need of the 450 biggest multinational corporations in the world. In their expanding global operations, these huge . . . companies have created the demand for free access to money across all borders. . . ."[17]

Alongside this development, which created a demand for Eurodollars, was another that provided the wherewithal for the growth of Eurodollar deposits. When Europe started to become saturated with dollars, the dollars no longer turned over rapidly in transactions but instead were deposited in banks. Now the private banks had another source of deposits to go along with the rather small sums acquired from Russia, Eastern Europe, and other relatively small Eurodollar depositors. Consequently, both the supply side (deposits) and the demand side (loans to multinationals) of the Eurodollar system found a happy marriage.

The first of what was to become a pattern of moves and countermoves by the regulators and the regulated occurred in 1963 and 1964 when the Kennedy and Johnson administrations imposed the Interest Equalization Tax. The tax added a cost both to international loans that originated in the United States for American multinationals and to borrowing in the United States by foreign companies. This was precisely the market that Eurodollars were made for, and the banks responded by making loans to American multinationals and foreign companies out of their Eurodollar deposits. Although not originally designed for this purpose, the large private international banks used the Eurodollar system to provide capital to U.S. multinational corporations who were trying to avoid the higher cost of borrowing in the United States. As the Congressional Joint Economic Committee puts it: "The motivation underlying the inception of the Eurodollar market was the desire to avoid regulation, either regulations already in effect or additional restrictions that depositors feared might be imposed."[18]

A new twist was also added in the mid-1960s that pushed the Eurodollar system toward further growth through institutional innovation. That new twist consisted of intrabank transfers and interbank borrowing. Intrabank transfers was a way in which banks could receive deposits in their U.S. branches, lend abroad, and avoid the Interest Equalization Tax. Rather than issue loans to multinationals from the United States and be subject to the Interest Equalization Tax, the banks simply transferred money from their New York headquarters to one of their offshore branches. Heretofore, the Eurodollar system had received deposits primarily from customers in other countries. Now the banks were taking dollars deposited in the United States and moving them abroad, thereby expanding the potential Eurodollar base to include deposits in the United States. The system was moving toward its full-fledged supranational maturity, although another decade would have to pass before this was reached.

To go along with intrabank transfers, there was another way of expanding Eurodollar deposits via interbank borrowing. Here a bank borrows from another bank and locates the borrowed dollars in one of its Euroaccounts. What emerges from these two new forms of Eurodollar expansion is a pyramid of credit with one bank linked to another. And like a chain, the system is only as strong as its weakest link. The Congressional study on banking in the mid-1970s points out that "one bank's problems are inevitably passed on to others [and] the failure of any one of these banks could cause the most serious disruption in financial markets not only in the United States, but in other countries as well."[19]

Like a Tom and Jerry cartoon-chase sequence, a new strategy is devised once the lumbering cat (the government) discovers it has been outwitted by the resourceful mouse (the supranational banks). In 1965, that new tactical move was the so-called "voluntary" credit controls that the Johnson administration used to jawbone U.S. multinationals into investing in the United States, instead of overseas. But all that happened as a result of this policy was that more loans were issued through the Eurodollar markets and outside of the regulatory reach of the U.S. authorities.

By the late 1960s, the ceiling on interest that banks could pay their customers under Regulation Q provided another impetus for large wealth-holders to transfer their dollars into Eurodollar accounts, where they could earn higher rates of interest. From a modest beginning of about $11 billion Eurodollars in 1964, the system had grown to $40 billion by 1969—measured conservatively.

I say "measured conservatively" because there are several different estimates of Eurodollars to choose among and they vary from the most restricted one I am using of $40 billion in 1969 to as much as $85 billion in that same year.[20] There are two basic sources for the Eurodollar statistics—the Bank for International Settlements in Basel, Switzerland, an international financial institution created by governments after World War I to perform some of the functions of an international bankers' clearing house, and the Morgan Guaranty Trust Company, a New York supranational bank. The BIS, as the Bank for International Settlements is known, provides statistics for a longer period of time and nets out interbank transactions. On the other hand, they have only recently started to include data from outside of Europe, and some of these offshore banking sanctuaries grew rapidly in the 1970s. Morgan includes all Eurodollar centers but has less-detailed breakdowns. The estimates in this chapter are all net of interbank transactions but include all Eurodollar centers; they also exclude currencies other than dollars.

Eurodollars remain outside of the regulatory authority of the United States government not because of any insurmountable technical problem in monetary policy. Eurodollars are beyond the government's regulatory reach because there has never been the political will to place them inside the jurisdiction of public policy. The supranational banks take the position that only the country that houses the Eurodollar deposits can regulate them. While chartered in the United States and hungry for taxpayer bailouts when they need them, American banks have effectively resisted regulation of their very profitable offshore activities. The supranationals are like children who run away from home because they do not want to submit themselves to Mommy's and Daddy's authority but return when they become hungry and want a meal.

"For many," writes *Business Week*, "the existence of an unregulated pool of lendable funds so big . . . is an elegant thing to behold. Stateless money is deposited and lent through banks in the Euromarkets with absolutely no bureaucratic interference. These banks hold no required reserves against deposits in case of a crisis in the future. And they have no insurance on deposits to push up costs."[21] Add to this the fact that the banks' processing costs are lower because they are dealing only with large deposit sums and large loans—not the nickels and dimes they have to bother with in your account and your home mortgage—and there is the possibility described by Morgan Guaranty Trust in which "banks are able to offer higher rates of interest to depositors and lower lending rates to borrowers" and still earn higher profits than they do on domestic accounts.[22]

The regulations that protect us as bank customers are the very ones whose absence makes the Eurodollar system so profitable for the banks. First among these regulations is the system of reserve requirements. Deposits in the United States require a reserve to be held against them in case a bank is in financial trouble. The amount of reserves is set by the Federal Reserve Board and typically hovers around 20 percent. When reserves are joined with the insurance on checking and savings accounts, the twin pillars of protection in the banking system are in place. Neither exists in the Eurodollar system.

The system of reserve requirements is not only an important protection for your money; it is also a means by which the Federal Reserve regulates the rate of growth of the American money supply. Here is how it works. For every dollar deposited in a bank, about 20 cents is held by the bank as a reserve and the balance of 80 cents is available to be lent out to borrowers. The 80 cents lent out by the bank provides dollars to its loan customers who probably will turn around and deposit this 80 cents either in the bank from which the money is borrowed or in some other bank. Now a new account of 80 cents has been created in the banking system, and again the bank has to hold 20 percent of this (16 cents) in reserve and can lend out a new 64 cents. This process is called the multiple expansion of money. The first dollar deposited creates money as it is lent out through the banking system. After the second round, for example, banks as a total system have $1.80, and after the third round $2.44

—the original dollar, the 80 cents after the first lending cycle, and 64 cents after the second. The first dollar deposited, in effect, turns over each time a portion of it is lent out and redeposited to create new deposits in the banking system. The process does not go on indefinitely because of the reserve requirement. At each stage in the cycle, a smaller amount is availaable to lend out, and quickly credit expansion atrophies as smaller and smaller amounts are available for new lending.

In the unregulated Eurodollar arrangement, however, there are no required reserves and, consequently, the potential expansion of money is theoretically unlimited. Eurodollars are different from dollar deposits inside the United States because "the banks are free to lend the entire amount on deposit," says H. Robert Heller, the head of Bank of America's international economics division.[23] To the banker, this is heaven; the dollar deposited can work for him to its fullest and a portion does not have to remain idle. This means "the Eurobanks will flourish," writes Robert Z. Aliber, an academic specialist in international finance, "as long as U.S. authorities permit the offshore branches of U.S. banks to operate with lower reserve requirements than the domestic offices."[24]

While an unlimited expansion of bank credit in the Eurodollar system is a theoretical possibility, in practice banks retain some Eurodollars as reserves, although they are far smaller than the reserves required on domestic deposits. And in two periods—1969–70 and 1979–80—the Federal Reserve Board placed reserve requirements on Eurodollar accounts—but only for a short period of time, until they succumbed to bank pressure to remove them. "Like all banks," says the Congressional report on banking, "Eurocurrency banks hold reserves. But, for the most part, they are exempt from mandatory reserves and this is very advantageous both in terms of profitability and flexibility," but "the result is a reduction in control by monetary authorities over the level of Eurocurrency activity."[25]

The institutional innovations of the 1960s ushered in the supranational banking era and the absence of reserve requirement regulations was the key. Gunter Dufey and Ian H. Giddy, professors at the University of Michigan's and Columbia University's schools of business, conclude in their study of Eurodollars: "When depositors shift from deposits in domestic banks to deposits in external banks, the total volume of credit extended rises because domestic deposits are subject to reserve requirements while the same deposits held in Eurobanks are not."[26] Susan Strange punctuates this conclusion with her own. Eurodollars "may prove to have been the most important single development of the century undermining national monetary sovereignty."[27]

Supranational Banks and Petrodollar Recycling

T HE TWO momentous world economic events of the 1970s—the end of Bretton Woods and the emergence of OPEC—pushed the adolescent supranational monetary order to maturity. When Bretton Woods folded its tent between 1971 and 1973, international monetary affairs became effectively deregulated. At the same time, the huge surpluses earned by OPEC on inflated oil prices filled Eurodollar coffers with a new source of funds that made previous deposits look like peanuts. Aided and abetted by the technological revolutions in information processing and communications, the great supranational banks inaugurated a new epoch in the world political economy.

After 1973, there was an explosion in the growth of Eurodollars and the source was the vast dollar surpluses acquired by the oil-producing countries. OPEC countries as a group had about $7 billion in surplus earnings in 1973. That means they earned nearly $7 billion more for the sale of their oil than they spent in the rest of the world. During 1974, and after the fourfold increase in crude oil prices, the surpluses were $68 billion—nearly ten times larger than the year before. The dollars came pouring into OPEC hands as fast as the oil gushed out of the sands of the Arabian desert.

The rate of inflow of dollars was so great that several of the OPEC nations could not spend the money fast enough. This was particularly true for the large oil producers with small populations: Saudi Arabia, Kuwait, and the United Arab Emirates. Iran was spending all it earned on military equipment and the shah's grandiose development schemes, and the smaller producers—Algeria, Libya, Nigeria, Indonesia, Venezuela, and the Caribbean producers—began spending their earnings in a year or two. What the few surplus-earning members of OPEC did with their new dollar wealth was place it in offshore branches of American banks in Eurodollar accounts. And as the 1970s unfolded, the surpluses continued: $35 billion in 1975, $40 billion 1976, and $30 billion in 1977.[28] All told, between 1974 and 1977 the surplus earnings were $173 billion. Virtually all of this went into the Eurodollar system and was then lent out to create an even further growth of world liquidity.

The supranational banks were delighted. Here was an enormous new source of deposits, and banks always want money deposited with them as their ads for your funds testify. The dollars were received from OPEC countries and placed outside of the United States where there were no regulations and minimal taxes. With no legal reserve requirements imposed on these deposits, the potential for earnings was unlimited, or so it appeared. There was even a new name coined for these OPEC earnings: petrodollars, and a name given to their circulation through the deposit and relending process, petrodollar recycling.

The huge acquisition of new Eurodollars, however, was a mixed blessing for the banks. They were paying interest on the large certificates of deposit to their OPEC customers, and the problem was to find lending outlets that could earn a higher rate of interest than the one paid on the petrodollars. The traditional loan recipients of Eurodollars, multinational corporations, could not absorb the tens of billions the banks needed to unload for two reasons. First, the worldwide recession soured prospects for new investments on the scale required. Second, even in the best of times, the multinationals could not profitably absorb that much money. Never in the history of the world has there been such a massive movement of wealth among countries in such a short period of time.

To fill this breach, new actors appeared on the world financial stage: less-developed countries (LDCs) in the Third World. The banks found their borrowers in governments who needed to take out loans to pay for the inflated price of oil and other inflation-driven commodities. "Before the 1970s," says the Congressional report *Financial Institutions and the Nation's Economy*, "the principal borrowers from U.S. banks' foreign branches were private corporations—mostly U.S. based multinationals—and foreign banks which used the funds to finance private borrowers in their domestic markets. In the early 1970's, loans to less developed countries were made in the form of direct loans to governments or central banks or loans to development institutions which carried actual or implied government guarantees."[29]

The supranational banks, eager to unload their new-found cornucopia of petrodollars, pushed money at LDCs in what can only be described as an imprudent manner. S. C. Gwynne, a twenty-five-year-old English M.A. with just eighteen months of banking experience, describes how he was thrown into this maelstrom:

The world of international banking is now full of aggressive, bright, but hopelessly inexperienced lenders in their mid-twenties. They travel the world like itinerant brushmen, fill-ing loan quotas, peddling financial wares, and living high on the hog. Their bosses are often bright but hopelessly inexpe-rienced twenty-nine-year-old vice presidents with wardrobes from Brooks Brothers, MBAs from Wharton or Stanford, and so little credit training they would have trouble with a simple retail installment loan.[30]

The recipients of this banking largesse were those LDC governments deemed credit-worthy—like Brazil, Mexico, or Taiwan—or those in a favored political cate-gory such as Zaire, Turkey, and the Philippines. In nearly all instances, the banks did not have to worry about finding willing borrowers in the Third World, whose political leaders were only too eager to mortgage their country's future for short-term political expe-diency. A select few resisted the temptation to borrow. "It wasn't easy," says Abdon Espinosa, former minister of economy for Colombia. "I suffered the siege of the bankers, too. We had money shoved at us from all sides. But we maintained our control. Now we are better off than almost anyone else."[31] Espinosa's reaction to the financial system's overload of the mid-1970s is con-firmed by Gwynne, who sat on the other side of the table: "As a domestic credit analyst, I was taught to de-velop reasonable asset security for all loans unless the borrower was of impeccable means and integrity. As an international loan officer, I was taught to forget about that, and instead to develop a set of rationales that would make the home office feel good about the loan, even though, technically, it was 'unsecured.' "[32] With Gwynne's job performance "rated according to how many loans you make," and not on their credit-worthiness, it is no wonder that so many bad loans were made by the supranational banks to the LDCs that cannot be repaid.

The first great burst of petrodollar recycling institutionalized a process that we are still living with—"billion[s] thrashing around the world, linked to no productive sequence and serving only speculation based on quick returns," writes the Mexican novelist and diplomat Carlos Fuentes.[33] After a year's hiatus with OPEC surpluses in 1978—there were only $2 billion in surpluses in that year—they started up again in 1979 ($68 billion) and peaked in 1980 ($114 billion), as oil prices tripled during the political instability in Iran that saw the shah fall and the ayatollah rise to power.[34] From the first oil price increase in late 1973 to the end-of-decade price increase, OPEC surpluses were $357 billion. This astounding sum of money represents earnings in the world economy by a handful of countries that could not be quickly respent and became part of a supranational privately controlled bank money.

For every dollar of surplus for one country in the world economy, there is a dollar of deficit for some other country; the global bookkeeping ledger nets out to zero. Those deficits must be met by borrowing. The World Bank reports that the total debt of the LDCs that import oil was nearly $400 billion by the end of 1979, with about half owed to private banks.[35] From a 1973 base of about $117 billion, Eurodollars grew to $425 billion by 1979.

The statistical circuit, therefore, by the end of the 1970s was complete: about $350 billions of OPEC surpluses; almost $400 billions of Third World debt; and a quadrupling of unregulated Eurodollars to $425 billion. And all of this happened in just seven years. The OPEC countries found an income-producing secure place for their excess earnings; Third World countries could stay alive economically—some just barely; the banks could earn handsome profits in an unregulated environment on the interest spread; and the supranational banking era reached a new plateau.

In retrospect, there is no doubt that the supranational banks did indeed keep the world economy afloat during the 1970s, in the face of enormous shocks to the system. The speed with which they recycled petrodollars was a sight to behold, assisted, of course, by the revolution in communications and information processing that fortunately became available in the 1970s. Either poor countries would suffer more if they could not borrow the dollars to pay for their higher import costs of oil and other basic products dependent on oil, such as fertilizer, or they could buy time through indebtedness. The banks responded with alacrity to the petrodollar recycling crisis, but at a price that now plagues the world economy. The authors of the Congressional FINE report on banking produced a balanced assessment of the 1970s: "While foreign activities of U.S. banks have no doubt aided the development of world trade, these activities have also posed important problems for domestic monetary policy and for the stability of the U.S. banking system."[36]

The New Offshore Supranational Banking Sanctuaries

P ANAMA is known for its canal and its hats; the Bahamas and Cayman Islands as sandboxes for the rich; Hong Kong and Singapore for their sweatshops. In the 1970s, however, these places also became the location for the fictional receipt of billions of petrodollar deposits and for the fictitious booking of billions in Eurodollar loans—"fictitious" because the money never really roosted there, except for the instant of time when it appeared as a bookkeeping entry on a computer tape in the New York headquarters of the supranational banks. Fearing a freeze on their accounts, the OPEC countries did not want their vast petrodollar surpluses to be vulnerable in any way whatsoever, and they insisted, therefore, on the safest venues for their Eurodollar accounts. The supranational banks wanted to avoid taxes and regulations that would inhibit the earning capacity of their newfound Eurodollar cornucopia. And several Third World countries obliged by providing the safe haven for both the banks and the OPEC depositors.

In the 1960s, the City of London was the prime location for Eurodollar activity, but it lost out to less-regulated enclaves in the 1970s because the British government started to regulate foreign banks, and in 1975 they imposed a tax on the earnings of foreign banks. The FINE report points out that

foreign banks pay taxes to the British government on income earned in London but pay no taxes to local authorities on profits earned in the Caribbean. Therefore, banks concentrate their necessary but minimally profitable interbank lending in London and their highly profitable lending to the external market in the Caribbean since this reduces the overall amount of foreign taxes paid.[37]

Subject to the whims of political-economic trends, the older European banking sanctuaries did not provide as free and protected a setting for the operations of supranational banks as did some of the emerging less-developed countries. According to a study by the Organization for Economic Cooperation and Development (OECD), there were 803 branches in the Third World offshore banking centers in 1978–79, compared with 875 in all of Europe and Great Britain.[38]

With modern computer technology coming on-line in the mid-1970s, it did not take long for these new offshore banking sanctuaries to become dominant players in the petrodollar recycling game. By the middle of the decade, some 31 percent of the assets of all the foreign branches of American banks were located in the two tiny Caribbean islands of the Bahamas and the Cayman Islands—a growth of more than 150 percent since 1973 —and by May of 1976 more offshore loans were recorded in the Caribbean than in London.[39]

The Caribbean banking business is worthy of Alice in Wonderland. In the Bahamas, there is one bank for every eight hundred inhabitants; row upon row of small cinder-block buildings dot the landscape. The logos of supranational banking empires appear on brass plaques in front of the buildings, but inside, says the *New York Times,* there is only a "license, a filing cabinet, and a desk."[40] In no other place in the world will you find "hundreds of . . . U.S. banks [with] branches in the same city," says Larry Kramer of the *Washington Post,* "in fact on the same block of that city . . . Bay Street in Nassau, the Bahamas . . . and in some cases even in the same office."[41] Citibank, with a staff in the

Bahamas characterized by the *New York Times* as "largely bookkeepers," is reported in 1976 to have booked about 20 percent of its offshore loans from the Bahamas and received deposits from Kuwait alone worth $1.25 billion.[42]

The expansion in the size of the offshore banking sanctuaries is a tribute to the institutional ingenuity of supranational bank managers and could not have happened with such alacrity without the coincident technological revolution in communications and information processing. Before OPEC's run-up in oil prices, Eurodollar deposits in the offshore banking sanctuaries were inconsequential. By 1976, they had grown to $133 billion and at the start of the next decade (1980), Eurodollar deposits were $325 billion. They continued to grow through the 1980s to the point where Eurodollar deposits in the tiny offshore banking sanctuaries reached the staggering sum of $512 billion by the end of 1984.[43]

The balance sheets and profit-and-loss statements of American banks began to mirror their institutional evolution toward supranational entities. In 1960, eight U.S. banks had branches in other countries; in 1965, only eleven. By 1975, however, some 125 American banks had 732 branches operating in fifty-nine foreign countries, which led the Congressional Committee on Banking, Currency, and Housing to say that "the current scale of U.S. banks' involvement in overseas activity is without historical precedent."[44] By the mid-1970s, the institutional infrastructure of the supranational banking system was largely in place and all that has occurred since are further refinements. The number of foreign branches, for example, grew more slowly after 1975 to about one thousand.[45]

The investment banking firm of Salomon Brothers says this "highly complex, sophisticated and unregulated market where multinational banks take, place, and redeposit Euromonies is larger than any domestic money market in the world," and "growth in international earnings . . . accounted for 95% of the total earnings increase" in the largest American banks between 1970 and 1975.[46] They go on to point out that earnings on international activities grew by 36 percent during this period while domestic bank earnings *declined* by 9 percent. In 1975, about two-thirds of the income of the twelve largest American banks originated in their foreign branches, says the Congressional FINE report— 82 percent for Chase Manhattan, 63 percent for First National Bank of Chicago, and 80 percent for First National Bank of Boston.[47]

Citibank: The Model Supranational Bank

T HE VERY model of a modern multinational monetary machine is America's second-largest bank, First National City Bank of New York, known better by the name of Citibank and described by Ann Crittenden of the *New York Times* in 1977 as the "most truly international bank in the world."[48] In 1982, *Business Week* reported that Citibank's thirty thousand "employees located in 1,490 offices in 94 foreign countries . . . generated 67 percent of its deposits and 60 percent, or $448 million, of its net income from abroad."[49] "When Citibank advertises that it never sleeps," says the economist Robert Heilbroner, "it speaks more literally than most people know. As evening comes to America, United States bank deposits are, in a sense, released from duty, because no transactions take place for which their tutelary presence is required.

Therefore, the out-of-service deposits are loaned overnight by Citibank and all other big banks to financial
centers such as Hong Kong or Singapore, where the
business day has just begun. There the deposits play
their formal role of backing credit transactions until the
sun sets in the Orient and the time comes for the funds,
like Cinderellas, to return to work in America."[50]

The genius behind Citibank's empire is Walter Wriston, who transformed it from a "New York bank with
some foreign branches . . ." into "a worldwide financial
institution," whose "strategy is not one of making
loans," but "of making money."[51] However, in a celebrated 1978 lawsuit by a former Citibank employee,
questions were raised about the propriety of some of the
ways in which Citibank made money.

David Edwards was twenty-eight years old when he
started working for Citibank's Paris office in 1974 as a
foreign exchange dealer, someone who buys and sells
currencies. In 1977, he charged Citibank with manipu-
lating foreign exchange transactions between the Paris
office and its Nassau branch so as to understate taxable
earnings in Europe and inflate profits in the tax-free
Bahamas. Edwards was fired in February of 1978 and
the Board of Directors of Citicorp—Citibank's parent
company—appointed Shearman & Sterling, its own
New York law firm to conduct an investigation. While
generally exonerating Citibank of any blatant illegal activity—as these internal reports by sympathetic retain-
ers tend to do—the report did conclude, according to
the *Wall Street Journal,* that "some of Citibank's for-
eign-exchange practices could land the bank in trouble
with European tax authorities."[52] Specifically, the aud-
itors said the currency transactions could "be a viola-
tion of the laws of . . . Zurich," and also "may be
inconsistent with [German law]."[53]

Foreign exchange transactions by American supranational banks are so large that they can affect the dollar's international value and, at times, contravene the policy direction of the American government. There was some conjecture that the large American banks participated in the 1977 run against the Carter dollar by exchanging their dollars for other currencies. If true, the supranational U.S. banks were simply playing against the dollar as the best way, in Wriston's words "of making money." With so many dollars managed by American banks in Eurodollar accounts, it is not an unlikely possibility, although the banks vehemently deny the allegation.

David Edwards raised this issue in an article he wrote for *MBA Magazine:* "The dollar does not fall. It is pushed. . . . Through foreign currency exchange dealers, who make up a fraction of the worlds's international banking community, banks trigger exchange rate movements for big profits."[54] Edwards's charge could be dismissed as the ramblings of a disgruntled employee who had been fired by Citibank. But the highly regarded commodity market newsletter, *Green's,* said about this same incident that "the American bankers . . . are the dollar's enemy number one."[55]

With so much "hot" money, as it is called, available to be moved at a second's notice, it stands to reason that profit-obsessed bankers would not permit their earnings profile to be undercut by a sharp fall in the dollar. They would protect themselves by moving their Eurodollars into other currencies, thereby worsening whatever speculative run there was against the dollar. "There is no effective watchdog on the rapidly growing business of international money trading," writes Larry Kramer, who followed these issues carefully in 1977 and 1978, "and there is a huge potential for abuse. In fact, the abuse need not be too sophisticated to be lost in the abnormally secret world of banking."[56]

International Banking Facilities: Reproducing the Cayman Islands in the United States

I F YOU can't beat 'em, join 'em. That seemed to be the public policy posture toward the supranational banks in the late 1970s and early 1980s, when a remarkable entity was created, called the International Banking Facility, or IBF for short. In effect, the IBF reproduces inside the United States an almost exact replica of the offshore banking sanctuary.

Since October 1, 1981, the Federal Reserve Board has permitted states to establish "enterprise zones" for banks, where the international activities of the banks are exempt from taxation, reserve requirements on their deposits, and government insurance on their deposits. Restricted to so-called "nonresident" activity, deposits could be received from U.S. or foreign individuals and corporations, but they had to be initiated from outside the country. Loans were treated in the same way; so long as they were received outside the United States, they could be made to American multinational corporations, U.S. citizens, or foreign citizens and corporations. These free trade zones permitted the banks to operate onshore as they had been doing offshore, with one minor technical exception: the onshore IBFs had to hold deposits for at least two days instead of the overnight waiting period offshore. Aside from this minor inconvenience, supranational banks were able to replicate inside the United States the favorable profit position they had developed offshore.

This provides a glimpse into an important new dimension of the supranational system: the import of economic policy from abroad. Normally, we think of imports and exports involving the movement of goods or services. But in the supranational epoch, there is also a lively international trade in economic and social policy. A weakened Carter administration, in the face of powerful extraterritorial monetary forces, opened up this possibility in 1978, when discussions about the IBFs began. Warnings at that time from people like Philip E. Coldwell, a member of the Fed's Board of Governors, went unheeded. "The problem is one of leakages," he said. "How do we maintain control of the money supply with a free trade zone?"[57] Led by Citibank, the supporters of the scheme countered that there were already leakages into the offshore centers and, besides, the IBFs would restore jobs inside the United States that had been moved abroad. When skeptical New York legislators raised questions about taxes that would be lost— estimated to be about $12.6 million in 1976—"supporters of the plan, . . . the major New York City banks," countered with the argument "that neither the state nor the city would lose any tax money since the foreign loan activities that would be exempted from taxation have already moved out of New York."[58]

By June of 1983, just twenty-one months after the start of IBFs, there were already over four hundred established in seventeen states and the District of Columbia—about half in New York.[59] Eurodollar deposits in the IBFs were $171 billion by mid-1983, roughly the same size as the total amount of time deposits in all savings and loan associations in the country.[60] U.S. financial regulators had effectively surrendered their sovereignty to supranational banks who imposed a financial regulatory policy that was imported from places like the Cayman Islands and overthrew decades of carefully constructed public safeguards.

The consequence of international monetary deregulation in the 1970s and the emergence of an unsupervised supranational monetary system was worldwide economic austerity in the 1980s, the rise of monetarism as a dominant conservative political-economic doctrine, and financial instability. This is how *Business Week* assesses the development of supranational banking: "The new banking order tremendously increases the efficiency of moving cash around the globe, and that very ease of shifting billions at a moment's notice makes currency instability chronic and dollar weakness inevitable."[61]

6

GLOBAL AUSTERITY

HE TEN-YEAR period after the collapse of Bretton Woods was like no other in previous U.S. economic history. The emergence of a supranational monetary order contributed to the economic turbulence that forced governments to ask people to fasten their financial seat belts until a more placid economic ride could be arranged. But each time the nation safely negotiated one economic obstacle, another arose. Until the end of the 1970s, the inflation story dominated the evening news, while at the start of the 1980s, the spending spree had given way to economic austerity that produced the highest rate of unemployment in the United States since the Great Depression.

From 1973 to 1984, consumer prices increased by 134 percent in the United States—a basket of goods and services that cost $100 in 1973 now sold for $234 in 1984. To put this in some perspective, during the entire twenty-seven-year Bretton Woods period, from 1946 to 1972, the overall rate of consumer inflation was only 114 percent. This high rate of inflation was a totally new experience for the country. Yet the United States had less inflation than other industrial countries, except for West Germany. The rate of inflation in the European Community, for example, was 187 percent between 1973 and 1984.[1]

While the industrial countries inflated their economies in response to OPEC price increases after the demise of Bretton Woods, Third World countries had to scurry around to find ways to maintain their rates of imports—both of oil from OPEC and other inflation-driven products purchased from the industrial countries. Those that could went into debt and borrowed some time, while others that could not gain access to private-bank credit reduced their living standards. From a total debt of a little over $100 billion in 1973, less-developed countries (LDCs) were in hock to the tune of nearly $900 billion by the end of 1984—$550 billion owed to private banks and the rest to governments and public international lenders, like the World Bank.[2] Third World countries were not alone in buying time with debt, however. The U.S. government accumulated as much national debt between presidents Gerald Ford and Ronald Reagan as had been amassed between George Washington and Gerald Ford. Everyone was trying to postpone facing their economic problems however they could—through inflation, international debt, national debt, or personal debt.

As the inflationary seventies gave way to the austere eighties, politics shifted from liberal to conservative, economics from Keynesian to monetarist, and the public mood about the future from confident to uncertain. Real economic growth averaged only 1 percent per year between 1980 and 1983 in the U.S., compared with about 2.5 percent each year from 1973 to 1979. The measured unemployment rate peaked at over 10 percent for almost a year between 1982 and 1983, while the actual rate, which includes those individuals who have dropped out of the labor force, was around 13 percent. The American economy recovered midway through 1983, but the recovery left a residual unemployed of over 7 percent of the work force in 1984, which would have been considered a recession rate of unemployment in the 1970s.

While disappointing, the United States' economic performance in the 1980s was better than the rest of the world. About eighteen million new jobs were created between 1973 and 1983 in the U.S. economy, while the ten member-countries of the European Community *lost* more than 3.5 million jobs.[3] The Organization for Economic Cooperation and Development (OECD) forecasts that one in four young people under twenty-five will be unemployed in Western Europe by the middle of 1986, while unemployment for the adult population is expected to increase from its present rate of just over 10 percent to 11.75 percent. Journalists have coined a new term for this bleak economic outlook: Europessimism. There is a "danger of adding a wholly new concept to the economic lexicon: the Revolution of Declining Expectations," says the British newspaper the *Observer*, in an editorial on Thatcher's economic policies in Great Britain.[4]

The picture was even grimmer in the oil-importing LDCs, where growth rates fell from a little over 5 percent per year between 1973 and 1979 to around 2 percent on average for each year from 1980 to 1984. This was just about equal to rates of population growth; on a per capita basis, therefore, the LDCs that import oil had zero economic growth. The worldwide epidemic of economic austerity resulted in international trade that "has been more sluggish since 1979 than during any comparable period since the Second World War," reports the Bank for International Settlements.[5] The British economic journalist William Keegan concludes that "economic policy has not only not been designed to secure expansion: it has been biased towards restriction."[6]

Nothing in anyone's economy seemed to work the way it used to. Labor productivity did not grow as fast as it used to grow, profits were not as high as business had come to expect, and governments could not govern their economies when faced with new supranational economic forces that were not even recognized. Out of this sense that economic forces were reeling out of control came a political shift from a growth and employment commitment to a developing consensus around anti-inflationary economic retrenchment.

No doubt the time had come to reassess economic policy and shift economic gears, to rationalize unproductive enterprise, and to make government's social programs more effective and less costly. But in the excessive fervor with what the economic historian Joseph Schumpeter calls the process of creative destruction—the weeding out of the inefficient during periods of economic retrenchment that prepares the stage for new bursts of economic progress—economic policy tended to go too far and threw out the baby with the bath water.

A Decade of International Debt

A "RECYCLERS' recession" is the phrase used by the *Economist* to describe the way in which petro-dollar recycling in the 1970s was transformed into global austerity in the 1980s. "The world is in recession," they say, "because its bankers overlent to inefficient borrowers. . . . Everybody's back was being scratched. Capitalist countries kept their banks and factories busier. The rest of the world got the goods and services it wanted, plus the credit to pay for them." But there was "one huge snag: the world's savings were badly invested everywhere from Turkey through Poland to Zaire. Bankers claimed that they had no choice but to on-lend money deposited with them. Few took much trouble checking how their loans were being used. A friendly handshake from the head of a state-owned steel company in any one of thirty countries in Latin America and Asia and Eastern Europe was usually good for $50m."[7]

How serious a threat to the banking system is this $900 billion world debt—over $800 billion owed by LDCs at the end of 1984 and the rest by Eastern European countries and the Soviet Union? There are conflicting points of view on this within the financial community. James Gipson, the head of a Beverly Hills investment counseling firm, thinks "the prospect that . . . a wave of defaults on foreign loans will destroy the international financial system so terrifies Western governments that they are rushing to save even the most imprudent of their own vulnerable bankers."[8] The bankers pooh-pooh such apocalyptic talk. Their position is described by Hobart Rowen this way: "They tend to agree that, yes, there is a huge debt burden in the developing countries. And some of them will admit that, yes, the banks' own eagerness to turn a profit helped to build up the debt. But, they say, we will muddle through."[9] Or, as a U.S. banker told *Business Week*, "There is a feeling that if you're still in business, still going, still alive, the problem can be handled over time. That if everyone sticks together, we'll all come out all right."[10]

The world finally took notice of the potential dangers of the explosive international debt situation in 1982 and

1983, ten years after the borrowing binge started. When Poland in 1981 stopped paying on its $27 billion debt, eyebrows were raised in the world financial community. Then, in August of 1982, Mexico—in debt for $87 billion—announced it could no longer meet its interest and principal payments, and the world's supranational bankers knew they could no longer keep a lid on this pressure cooker that had been building up steam for nearly a decade. Mexico was followed in quick succession by Argentina, $37 billion, and finally by the biggest debtor of all and deemed the most credit-worthy of any LDC borrower: Brazil, $92 billion in debt in 1983. All told, among these four countries, a total of $243 billion was at stake and annual interest payments that make up a significant proportion of the earnings of the largest banks in the world. According to the Washington-based Institute for International Economics, the debt owed by Brazil and Mexico alone to the nine largest U.S. banks exceeds the total capital of these banks.[11]

Norman A. Bailey, as special assistant to President Ronald Reagan for national security affairs, played an important role in the U.S. government's response to this financial crisis, and he has said there was "an unwillingness to believe in the seriousness of events, their generalized character and possible consequences or the necessity or even desirability of advance contingency planning. When the situation finally erupted in acute form (August, 1982) crisis response was superb but entirely tactical. . . ."[12] It followed a script that had been used as early as 1972 in Bolivia. A grand game of chicken was played out and everyone watched to see who would flinch first. But the outcome was never really in doubt because the banks, as *Business Week* puts it, had "waltzed blithely into certain loans, particularly foreign ones, on the assumption that some official body— either central banks acting as lenders of last resort or

. . . agencies such as the IMF—would eventually bail them out."[13]

As the saying goes, if you owe your banker a little bit of money, it's your problem. But if you owe him a huge amount of money, it's his problem. The debts among the three Latin American debtors were so large, and the threat of some form of debtors' cartel so frightening, that a solution acceptable to the debtor countries was inevitable, though not before the usual game of financial brinkmanship had run its course.

The IMF as World Monetary Sheriff

W HEN LDC debt cannot be repaid, the IMF is cued in and takes center stage. The old trouper from the Bretton Woods touring company offers to lend a little bit of money to the debtor nation, which can then be leveraged into larger amounts of private-bank lending, on condition that it be permitted to monitor economic developments inside the country.

A characteristic feature of the supranational era is the desire of banks to be removed from regulatory authority but to come under a governmental security blanket when they are in trouble. "The banks want to be assured," says William H. Rhodes of Citibank, "that the country is going to be pursuing the necessary adjustment programs to take it out of its external debt situation to monitor what it's doing. The banks have found this a very difficult role to play as a group and felt that a multinational agency like the International Monetary Fund is better equipped to do so. . . ."[14] Rhodes and other supranational bankers had learned a bitter lesson in Peru in 1977, when they took on the burden of defining the conditions for a Peruvian debt rescheduling. *Business Week* cautioned at the time that such private bank activities "raise troublesome questions about foreign business interference in the affairs of a sovereign state."[15] After the Peruvian debacle, the banks worked out a new strategy that used the IMF as point man: "Though it was never articulated in so many words," says Pierre Latour, a European banking analyst, "most bankers must . . . have assumed that loans lent to LDC governments would be underwritten by the official aid programmes of the developed world. No Western government had any wish to see a debtor country default, or to inflict a major loss on its own banking system."[16]

Using what Arthur Burns, former head of the Federal Reserve Board and President Reagan's ambassador to West Germany, calls a "certificate of good standing"— known technically as a Stand-By Arrangement—the IMF provides an umbrella of security that is the key to opening up a renegotiation of the debt between private banks and the country that is in arrears on its debt payments.[17] This process is called *rescheduling*: new loans are provided by the private bankers that wipe out the old loans, but at a cost to the borrower. The cost is higher interest charges on the new loans and rescheduling fees that have to be paid up-front to the banks. When pressed about these large rescheduling fees and high interest rates, William H. Rhodes, senior vice president of Citibank in charge of Latin American debt negotiations, defended them by saying: "The initial arrangement [with Mexico] was done not because the banks were greedy or trying to prop up their balance sheets, but because they were very preoccupied that this would be a hard sell to the international banking community at large if you did not have high spreads and fees."[18]

The rescheduling fees and higher interest charges are

not the only costs; debtor countries mortgage some of their economic sovereignty when they enter into a Stand-By Arrangement, and American taxpayers pay for the bank bailout when Congress approves more money for the IMF. The Fund imposes economic austerity upon the debtor country as a condition for the Stand-By Arrangement, and this is a further cost in reduced economic growth for everyone in the world economy.

The IMF takes the view that debt is due to internal economic mismanagement, where countries have tried to live beyond their means and buy more in the world economy than can be justified by their export-earning potential. As a truism, this proposition is hardly debatable. By definition, a country borrows when it spends more in the world economy than it earns. And if at some point the nation cannot pay its debts, then it must have spent too much in the world economy in relation to what it can earn. But truisms do not necessarily make for good analyses nor are they appropriate guides for public policy.

The debt problem is largely global and structural in character, while the IMF sees it as endemic to a particular country and caused by poor economic management. It is the end result of a supranationalization process that started with international monetary deregulation between 1971 and 1973 and continued with the proclamation from the world's largest debtors in the early 1980s that they could not meet their payments without billions in additional loans. Norman A. Bailey, the Reagan administration insider, acknowledges this in his candid retrospective: "The international financial crisis . . . is the disease, which has been raging since the late sixties. [The LDC debt crisis] is one of the symptoms of the disease. Symptomatic treatment is a necessary but not sufficient element of the cure. . . ."[19]

The IMF's symptomatic remedy for whatever ails any

debt-ridden LDC is a combination of free-market monetarism and economic deflation. Its austerity regimen for
the more than forty LDCs that come under its economic
surveillance involves:

- currency devaluation to discourage imports and
  encourage exports;
- reductions in government expenditures (particularly for social programs);
- reductions in the rate of growth in the money supply;
- restrictive labor policies that reduce the rate of
  growth in real wages;
- freeing of prices from government regulation;
- easing of restrictions on foreign investment; and
- shift in income distribution from lower-income to
  higher-income groups in order to encourage savings and discourage consumption.

While denying this IMF strategy, applied to nearly one-
third of the countries in the United Nations, is one of
economic austerity, Jacques de Larosière, the Fund's
managing director, says that "the objective of restoring
a viable balance of payments position within a reasonable period of time implies that you must reduce your
domestic consumption, increase your domestic savings,
and expand your exports."[20] Most observers, outside of
the IMF organization, however, have no trouble calling
a spade a spade. The *Economist,* for example, says "a
country that cannot borrow generally has to trim its
deficit by deflating demand. That shaves a whisker off
world growth, adding to everybody's difficulties. As
recession spreads, more companies and countries are
finding that their botched investment cannot produce
the returns needed to service their debt."[21]

A little-known fact is that once a country gets hooked
on the IMF, it is hard to break the habit. The IMF medi-

cine, however, is as addictive as the loan disease it is supposed to cure. More than fifteen countries have had ten or more Stand-By Arrangements with the Fund in the past thirty years. Peru leads the pack with nineteen, followed by Haiti with eighteen, the Philippines and Liberia with sixteen, Panama with fifteen, six countries with thirteen, and so on.[22] Between 1975 and 1984, the private supranational banks have conducted over one hundred reschedulings involving fifty countries; Zaire alone has had six reschedulings in these nine years. In the crisis years of 1983 and 1984, the total amount of rescheduled debt was over $150 billion.[23]

This very high rate of recidivism among debt-rescheduled countries stems from the fact that the public policy community is not prepared to deal with the problem in a global context. Every borrower from the IMF is told to reduce its imports and expand its exports, while at the same time restraining purchasing power. If you stop and think for a moment, however, how can all countries reduce their spending power, yet sell more to other countries? Who can buy the exports if demand is contracting worldwide? Senator Bill Bradley (D-New Jersey) calls this the "paradox of austerity." "If everyone is adopting austerity measures," he asks rhetorically, "where will the growth stimulus come from?"[24] What may be good for one country in the world economy adds up to bad policy for that country and all others if enough nations follow the same policy. By restraining demand and purchasing power, the IMF has left the world economy without the ability to grow, which is a precondition for solving the debt problem.

This is a fundamental problem with free-market monetarism—a theory that says countries must pass through a process of economic hardship before the economic system can again function effectively. Harry Taylor, president of Manufacturers Hanover Corporation, a large New York bank with one of the heaviest exposures in Latin America, is concerned that "you get to the stage where the additional impact of monetarism gives you smaller and smaller returns in terms of reduction in inflation at a bigger and bigger cost in terms of the level of unemployment and the dislocation in the industrial and financial system."[25]

The issue of Third World debt is manifestly complex; there are no simple answers, no good guys and bad guys, and no easy exit from the labyrinthian character of the problem. The muddlers-through who have kept the world's financial system afloat deserve credit for a situation, says the economist Leonard Rapping, "that everybody knew had endgame difficulties."[26] The IMF was reluctantly thrust into a role of intruding itself into national economic policies that spawned a whole genre of political graffiti. In 1984, Margot Hornblower of the *Washington Post* saw signs on the walls in what she describes as the "poverty-stricken barrios of Santo Domingo" saying: "IMF, get out of our country."[27] (I recall arriving in Jamaica in the late 1970s and seeing "IMF" scrawled on walls. My taxi driver told me this stood for "Is Manley's fault"—referring to the democratic-socialist prime minister at the time.)

The U.S. government has had to play the role of lender-of-last-resort—more precisely, the American taxpayer has been forced into this role. The administration of whatever party is placed in an awkward position when it goes to Congress and says it cannot afford to expand student-loan programs in one breath and in another asks for a loan program for private supranational banks, laundered through the International Monetary Fund. The rationale for this arrangement is explained by a *Business Week* comment that "loans to countries have been viewed as 'evergreen' because of continuous rollovers and government reluctance to take the 'bankruptcy option.' "[28]

While the debate goes on about who is to blame for the debt crisis and what to do about it, one fact is clear: "Perhaps most damaging is the loss of credibility among international bankers," says Lawrence Rout of the *Wall Street Journal*. "There is a sense of shock at what has happened," he quotes an officer of a large New York bank who goes on to say that "people didn't quite understand how bad things were."[29] But did the world banking community really learn anything in 1983? A few months after the 1983 crisis, the Philippines—one of the world's great recidivists—came close to default. In exasperation, Hobart Rowen, the distinguished financial journalist of the *Washington Post* who has followed debt crisis after debt crisis over the past ten years, said: "The scary thing about the Philippines' crisis is the way it sneaked up on the presumably sophisticated financial community, despite the millions of words that have been written and spoken about Third World debt problems."[30]

By the end of 1984, Argentina had finally agreed to IMF conditions for private debt rescheduling after nearly a year of haggling. With the Mexican and Brazilian reschedulings in place, the world's financial community bought a few more years of breathing space and could justifiably pat themselves on their collective backs for a difficult job, well done. The handling of the 1983–84 crisis confirmed the banking community's view, as expressed in 1982 by Irwin L. Kellner, senior vice president of Manufacturers Hanover, that "the underlying economic and financial circumstances . . . do not justify the atmosphere of alarm that the media appear to be generating."[31] But what will happen during the next debt crisis? How many times can the financial community go to the same well? "The greatest article of faith" in the banking world, writes the *Guardian*'s financial columnist, Peter Rodgers, "is that two years after triumphantly muddling through since the Mexican crisis, the whole problem can be solved by more of the same feeble policy."[32] This proposition will be tested between 1984 and the end of 1987, when about half of all LDC debt—$277 billion—comes due.[33]

The Triumph of Monetarism

A LL THE financial forces unleashed in the 1970s joined together to produce free-market monetarism in the 1980s. Third World debt, the movements of unregulated supranational money, and the Eurodollar overhang created a political-economic momentum that no government, whether liberal or conservative, could ignore. Runs on the dollar that started as early as 1960 and continued until 1979 were the economic body's way of discharging some of its toxins, and high interest rates were the system's way of telling policy makers that the world economy was unhealthy. For a fever, a doctor can prescribe symptomatic medicines that suppress the temperature for a while and take the risk that the natural healing process of the body will defeat the disease. This is what economists—who believe in a comparable sort of natural equilibrium—have been advising governments to do for nearly two decades: treating symptoms, not causes, and hoping for an organic corrective process that never occurred. It was President Jimmy Carter's mistake to follow this prescription, as his predecessors had done, except that during his term, the illness had reached the critical stage. This is what forced his administration to surrender to Paul Volcker's monetarism in the fall of 1979.

Paul Volcker, recently appointed head of the Federal Reserve Board, arrived in Belgrade on the first of October 1979, cigars in hand, ready to join his counterparts from around the globe at the annual meetings of the World Bank and International Monetary Fund. Each fall, the world's most powerful financial figures meet in opulent surroundings to contemplate the monetary fate of the globe. Private supranational bankers chat with each other—no nasty antitrust laws impede direct communication among financial competitors—and central bankers mingle with international financial bureaucrats to discuss the world's financial future, while a private banker stops by to eavesdrop with no hint of governmental concern about collusion. The world of supranational banking is like no other in the commercial realm, because it is not encumbered by antitrust regulation of the sort applied to other business people who would suffer the full weight of antitrust prosecution if discovered at such a gathering.

The 1979 Belgrade conference was unique, however, because of the crisis surrounding the world's reserve currency. The dollar had been falling in value; it was down almost 20 percent from 1977, when Jimmy Carter took office. Eurodollar accounts amounted to nearly $1 trillion, and the Eurodollar depositors, not wanting to see their wealth depreciated, were moving dollars into gold, Swiss francs, German marks, and Japanese yen. Even American banks were reported to be doing this, thereby playing against their own country's currency. The usual way of handling such problems, that of having the Germans buy dollars and the Japanese stay put, had run its course and no longer was enough to postpone dealing with this international financial crisis.

There were no flies on the walls of the hotel suites to report about the private conversations among the central bankers in Belgrade, but from subsequent events it is not difficult to piece together the story. Volcker and the American delegation (which included the treasury secretary, William Miller) were confronted with the most serious warnings from the private and central bankers gathered in Belgrade—as Lindley H. Clark, Jr., of the *Wall Street Journal* puts it: "foreigners were telling [Volcker] the error of our ways."[34] Volcker returned to the United States, as Hobart Rowen reported at the time, "without even waiting for the first plenary session. . . ." The official reason given by Anthony Solomon, under secretary of the treasury, was that "he felt he could do more useful work in Washington."[35] No truer obfuscating public relations statement could have been concocted. Volcker returned to the United States to line up administration support for the monetarist strategy designed to prevent the dreaded free-fall in the dollar.

An event that came to play such an important part in people's lives was missed by everyone as it developed. The press, which was preoccupied with the pope's visit to the United States and an alleged Russian brigade in Cuba, focused mainly on rumors that Volcker was either about to resign or was in ill health. On October 6, with the full support of the Carter administration and before the world's financial movers-and-shakers could return to their computer screens, Volcker announced a new policy of monetarism. Henceforth, the Federal Reserve Board would target the rate of growth of the money supply, bring that money supply growth-rate down, take immediate steps to raise interest rates, and let the economic chips fall where they may. The Carter administration announced its complete support for these policies.

The high interest rates lowered the floodgates. Dollar holders could now comfortably stay with them, because the dollars could earn substantial returns—indeed, higher returns than could be acquired from any other currency or gold. In effect, the high interest rates are a bribe that says stay with the dollar because it earns a very high rate of return and carries limited risk. If the dollar holders can be made to believe in the long-term nature of the program, then the run against the dollar would be stemmed. This is why the Carter administration's support was so critical. Volcker alone could not have pulled off this ploy and made it believable to a skeptical audience.

The monetarism announced on October 6 was a departure from the standard Keynesian policy that had been followed by previous Federal Reserve Boards. The difference is technical but also has significant political implications. A monetarist policy targets the rate of growth of the money supply and, coupled with free markets, demands that both government policy and private actors in the economy adjust. Keynesian monetary policy targets interest rates and permits the money supply to grow to accommodate the private sector of the economy and the public policy objectives of government. One policy strategy—monetarism—demands adaptation from government and the private sector to the monetary authorities; the other—Keynesianism—demands adaptation from the monetary authorities to government policy and private economic developments.

With the triumph of monetarism, the supranational economic order was now able to impose conditions not only on private citizens and foreign governments, but on the U.S. government as well. The prime rate of interest—that rate charged by the largest banks to their most credit-worthy customers—soared to a peak of 21.5 percent fourteen months after Volcker's announcement. While there are varied and complex reasons for this run-up in interest rates, none was more compelling than the need to stop the dollar's fall in value in the world economy. And the need to do this is part of a larger story that involves the emergence of a supranational monetary order, operating outside of public authority, with its attendant explosion of stateless money and international debt.

The consequences of not treating global problems globally is described by Adam Raphael of the *Observer* as "sado-monetarism"—an apt term for a policy that has contributed to economic distress in the eighties.[36] "Every half-point climb in the [interest] rate increases debt costs to the cash-strapped borrower nations by about $2.5 billion a year," says James L. Rowe, Jr., of the *Washington Post*.[37] The dollar has soared in value, drawing wealth from other countries, and "rather than risk a disastrous fall in the value of marks and francs as a consequence of this currency flight," writes the economist Robert Heilbroner, "European banking authorities sought to counter the suction of high American rates by instituting tight-money policies of their own."[38]

The international trade in economic and social policy, characteristic of the supranational era. took on a new twist as the United States exported free-market monetarism to the rest of the world through its support for the IMF's conditionality in the Third World and its monetarist and free-market policies at home. The dollar's falling value of 1979 was replaced by its opposite in the 1980s, and "when the dollar rises," H. Erich Heinemann of the *New York Times* points out, "foreign governments are forced to 'defend' their currencies from falling by keeping interest rates higher than otherwise would be the case. The trouble with this medicine is that even when it works, it has unpleasant side effects—namely it acts to hold down economic activity."[39] The wild ride of the dollar in the past ten years over turbulent seas is attributed by *Business Week* to "the establishment of a supranational banking system that greases the path of money movements [but] also creates a vicious cycle of currency instability."[40]

At a time when the world's financial problems cried

out for visionary leadership, its leaders were more interested in narrow ideological struggles to restore the profitability of capital, as exemplified by this lengthy exegesis by Jacques de Larosière, head of the IMF, in a major policy address delivered in 1984:

Over the past four years (1980–1983) the rate of return on capital investment in manufacturing in the six largest industrial countries averaged only about half the rate earned during the late 1960s. . . . even allowing for cyclical factors, a clear pattern emerges of a substantial and progressive long-term decline in rates of return on capital. There may be many reasons for this. But there is no doubt that an important contributing factor is to be found in the significant increase over the past twenty years or so in the share of income being absorbed by compensation of employees. . . . This points to the need for a gradual reduction in the rate of increase in real wages over the medium term if we are to restore adequate investment incentives. . . .[41]

Setting aside the problem with the statistics de Larosière cites—most of the increase in the share going to labor is not because of higher wages but is due to the fact that there are simply more people who receive their income today from employment than there were in 1960, when there were many more sole proprietors of businesses and farm owners[42]—it is a rather remarkable preoccupation for an individual in his position, with the intellectual resources at his disposal in the vast international organization he directs.

The Fragility of the Banking System

A LL THIS talk of austerity may seem at odds with the American celebration in 1984 that started with the Hollywood-hype Olympics and ended with Ronald Reagan being swept back into office in a landslide. But the euphoria over an admittedly robust economic recovery was premature for two reasons: first, the recovery topped off at a level of unemployment that previously would have been considered a recession trough. And, second, the deindustrialization of the American economy, hastened along by the overvalued dollar, left the economy with a two-tier labor force: highly paid functionaries of the supranational economy and lower-paid jobs that service this system. Missing were the new middle-class industrial jobs that offer a young person an entry into stable employment at decent wages. A cartoon caption in the *Guardian,* the British daily newspaper, sums it up: "People Aren't Working, But the Economy Is."[43]

Lurking behind this illusory economic miracle was a banking system that was as delicately balanced as a high-wire act. Between 1982 and 1984, there were about 150 bank failures, in contrast to the 6 to 10 per year during the 1960s and 1970s. Only during the depths of the Great Depression was there a similar three-year period of bank insolvencies in this century (between 1936 and 1938 there were a little over two hundred bank failures).[44] In addition to the outright bank failures, William M. Isaac, chairman of the Federal Deposit Insurance Corporation, disclosed that there were 797 banks in 1984 "listed by . . . three federal banking agencies as problem institutions requiring special supervision"—"more than twice the peak reached after the 1973–75 recession. . . ."[45] And this does not take into account what the economist Michael J. Boskin describes as the way in which "government agencies have . . . made liberal use of creative accounting to keep institutions apparently solvent many years after they became fundamentally *insolvent*."[46]

What bankers fear most is a run on their bank, when depositors lose confidence and withdraw large sums of cash from their accounts. Sometimes the run forces the bank to close its doors; other times the bank survives but at the expense of its credibility. From the Great Depression to 1980, there was only one major run on an American bank: Franklin National Bank's run in 1974, which precipitated the largest American bank failure in over thirty years. Between 1980 and 1984, however, there were five large runs on major banks: First Pennsylvania (1980), $925 million; Greenwich Savings Bank (1982), $430 million; First National Bank of Seattle (1983), $900 million; First National Midland of Texas (1983), $800 million; and the whopper—Continental Illinois (1984), $15 billion.[47] The *Wall Street Journal* reporters who compiled these statistics point to two contributing factors: the enormous concentration of deposits in a few hands that feeds any speculative run on a bank and the fact that "large depositors . . . have access to modern-day telecommunications networks that carry news and rumors faster and farther than ever."[48]

The $7.5 billion bailout of Continental Illinois, the nation's eighth-largest bank, in 1984 was only the latest installment paid on the government's financial commitment to prop up the supranational banking system. It began ten years earlier with Franklin National Bank, a major international bank based on Long Island that ranked among the top twenty in size in the United States. Franklin, like its German counterpart, Bankhaus Herstatt, which also found itself in difficulty at about the same time, thought it would make a killing in the new deregulated foreign exchange markets. The only problem was that it misjudged who would be the victim. With about 30 percent of its total deposits offshore in London and Nassau, Franklin was the epitome of the new breed of supranational bank: brash, innovative, and overextended in chancy foreign loans. Between May and October of 1974, nearly $3 billion was withdrawn from Franklin—about a third from its offshore deposits —and the bank was forced to close its doors.[49] Herstatt, also shoulder-deep in risky foreign dealings, shut down at about the same time. The shock waves that rippled through the world's financial boardrooms were only a hint of what was to come later. But for the depositors in Franklin, and its other creditors who did not have the foresight to act in time, it was years of anxious waiting before their claims were adjudicated.

Iran and the Great Eurodollar Chase

T HE NEXT great wave of uncertainty after the collapse of Franklin and Herstatt in 1974 occurred during the Iranian hostage crisis of 1979–80, when the freezing of about $11 billion of Iranian deposits in U.S. banks, according to *Business Week*, shook the "international banking system around the world . . . [and] led to bitterness in the usually decorous international banking community, illustrating just how fragile the system is."[50] When Iran's foreign minister, Abolhassan Bani-Sadr, announced on November 14, 1979, that Iran would withdraw its money from American banks, the Carter administration countered with a pre-emptive strike of its own: a freeze order on all Iranian accounts in U.S. banks. Little did they know at the time that their actions would highlight the tension between the regulatory reach of the nation-state and the supranational operations of global banks.

Most of the Iranian deposits were in offshore Eurodollar accounts and presumably beyond the regulatory authority of the American government. The banks, after all, had been assuring their OPEC depositors over and over again that accounts held outside of the United States could not be touched by American law. But here was an instance where the banks chose to honor the freeze order and effectively proclaim Nassau, London, the Cayman Islands, and all the other offshore banking sanctuaries within the regulatory jurisdiction of the U.S. government and no longer a safe haven for foreign accounts under any and all circumstances.

This so disturbed the other Arab OPEC countries, reported *Business Week,* that William Miller, Carter's treasury secretary had to make a special four-day trip to the Middle East "to soothe the unexpected anger of Arab oil producing countries over the U.S. freeze of Iran's financial assets."[51] Karin Lissakers, the deputy director of the State Department's Policy Planning staff at the time of the freeze, has remarked that "it was this extraterritorial reach that other governments found most troubling about the freeze order."[52] It was Bani-Sadr's understanding that "our funds are deposited in subsidiaries of U.S. banks, particularly in France, Britain, West Germany, and Switzerland. I am sure those countries will not allow such an illegal step to be taken."[53] He was wrong.

David Rockefeller, as president of Chase Manhattan and the shah's personal banker, played a key role in the maneuverings surrounding the Iranian bank accounts, just as he was instrumental in persuading Carter to permit the shah to enter the United States for medical treatment, which was the proximate event that triggered the taking of American hostages. "In London the air crackled with crisis," said *Business Week* at the time, as Iran's central bank "unleashed a blizzard of writs before the London high court. . . ."[54] Morgan Guaranty Trust Company obtained a court order in Germany that permitted it to attach Iranian assets held by a German bank that was part of a loan syndicate led by Morgan. The Nassau branch of the French bank Crédit Lyonnais froze $18 million in Iranian deposits for the same reason. Treasury Secretary William Miller took the position that "these are U.S. entities"—referring to the American banks—" and . . . we can freeze [Iranian] assets anywhere in the world."[55] However, the contradiction between nationalism and supranationalism was put more succinctly by Wilfried Guth, chief executive of the Deutsche Bank: "For an international bank, the departure from the international stage in order to assume temporarily a pure national role is not compatible with the degree of interdependence reached in the Eurocredit market."[56]

At the time, ten days after the taking of the hostages, the Iranian asset freeze was seen as a necessary measure to preserve the solvency of American banks. Six months later, however, the frozen Iranian accounts became the only tangible bargaining chip the United States had to use against the ayatollah. And when he became short of cash to prosecute his war against Iraq, the bankers and their frozen accounts played a central role in the ultimate exchange of hostages for the money sequestered in American banks. The first contact occurred in May 1980, when Iran's German lawyer got in touch with Citibank's lawyer in West Germany. Between that date and the final release of the hostages on January 20, 1981, there were almost continual negotiations that boiled down to a ransom: the unfreezing of Iranian accounts in exchange for the hostages. The haggling continued until the eleventh hour and nearly upset the planned exchange scheduled for Carter's last day in office. Finally, on Inauguration Day, 1981, the hostages were released and the bank accounts unfrozen. "It was an exchange of people and money unparalleled in the history of ransoms," writes Anthony Sampson. "The bankers had been at the center of the bargaining from the beginning, negotiating as if they were an independent state."[57]

President Jimmy Carter's memoirs provide a detailed and startling account of the asset freeze—which he concedes "stretched my legal authority to the limit"—and the role that the banks played in the drama that eventually freed the hostages.[58] Carter's problem, according to Karin Lissakers, was that "the U.S. government could lift the freeze order. . . . But it could not undo actions taken by some banks in the wake of the freeze. . . . The U.S. government therefore felt it was necessary to meet at least the minimum demands of the banks in the hostage agreement."[59]

Consequently, Carter was embroiled in two sets of negotiations, one with the Iranians and the other with the American banks. At times it was not clear which was the more difficult set of negotiations. "Ten of the banks had been cooperating," says Carter, "but at times . . . I had been angered because the Bank of America and one smaller bank seemed to be trying to compensate for unwise investment policies by claiming income from the Iranian deposits which they had not earned."[60] Robert Carswell, deputy secretary of the treasury, described the discussions with the banks taking place "in kind of a Quaker meeting atmosphere," but "less peaceful."[61]

Carter had become a middleman in the negotiations, an arbitrator between Iranian claims and the American supranational banks. At issue was the assurance that all the deposit accounts would be unfrozen; eventually, the two sides agreed to release $8 billion and permit the banks to keep $3 billion against Iranian claims that were in the courts and in the process of adjudication. A related issue was whether Iran would pledge to drop all future claims against the banks. A compromise was reached that defined the boundaries for future claims. The banks and Iran disagreed over how much interest should be paid on the frozen accounts. The banks claimed a minimal amount, since the funds had been idle and not earning interest income, while Iran wanted to be paid interest at the market rate for the period of time the funds were frozen. And, finally, all the other countries that were caught up in the legal entanglements had to be brought along in the final stages of the negotiations.

It literally came down to the final hours and minutes of Carter's presidency. He had hoped to conclude negotiations and have the hostages transferred on the day before he left office. Everything was ready. The planes were fueled in Tehran and about to fly off with the hostages to Algeria, whose foreign minister played a critical role in the negotiations. However, the Bank Markazi, the Iranian central bank, "would not issue the necessary papers," Carter writes in his memoirs. "I began to criticize the Iranian bank executives, only to discover that they were justified in not agreeing to the terms. . . . The planes were returned to standby condition. The Americans, presumably, were back in their prison."[62]

President Carter and most of his staff had a sleepless night before Inauguration Day, January 20, 1981. The graphic minute-by-minute account by Carter comes from his notes written during those fateful hours.[63] At 1:50 A.M.: "The machine is burping," reports the Treasury, referring to the telex connection with Tehran. "The bank Markazi was to send specific instructions to each of the twelve banks authorizing the transfer of exact amounts of principal and interest. . . ." 2:23 A.M., from the Treasury: "The message is moving." 2:40 A.M.: "The message is . . . garbled." 2:45 A.M.: "Serious difference has now developed among Americans . . . between

Treasury and the Federal Reserve." 3:05 A.M.: "Tell the banks to move using the garbled text," says Carter. 3:16 A.M.: "I instruct Miller [treasury secretary]: 'Order all American officials to conform to my position.' " 4:20 A.M.: "I listen to an unbelievable argument between New York and Algiers, with one of the irate Federal Reserve attorneys in Algeria finally saying that he is fainting and cannot discuss subject any further!" 4:38 A.M.: "Get Solomon [head of the New York Federal Reserve], Christopher [of the State Department], and the lawyers on the same line. I will use all the authority I have to get this resolved." 5:00 A.M.: "Finally, Solomon tells his attorneys, 'Sign it!' I breathe a sigh of relief."

Between five and ten in the morning, the final i's were dotted and t's crossed. The hostages were on their way to freedom, the banks had transferred exactly $7,977 billion to the Iranian central bank in five hours, and the nation awaited the inauguration of Ronald Reagan. At 10:45 A.M., Rosalynn Carter walked into the Oval Office to tell her husband: "Jimmy, the Reagans will be here in fifteen minutes. You will have to put on your morning clothes and greet them," while at the Treasury offices, down the street from the White House, William Miller recalled the scene: "The Reagan crowd, celebrating their moment, arrived in mink stoles to eat caviar and drink champagne in one end of the building, while we, unshaven and bleary eyed, waited at the other for word that the planes were finally taking off."[64]

This remarkable drama, that ended one of the most extraordinary events in modern diplomatic history, came down to the "banks themselves, not the U.S. government [negotiating] the financial terms of the hostage agreement," says Karin Lissakers, who was in a key State Department role during the negotiations with the banks.[65] The tensions between the nation-state and the supranational banking system had been exposed: "By freezing assets held in foreign branches of American banks, the U.S. government not only violated traditional rules of national sovereignty," argues Lissakers, "but also challenged the supranational status that the Euro-currency operations of private banks had always enjoyed."[66] Left unresolved, however, was the question of "which country has legal jurisdiction over a Euromarket operation."[67]

And what should we make of the spectacle of a president of the United States waiting for the approval from private banks and Federal Reserve lawyers before American diplomatic personnel can be liberated from the clutches of a tyrant who held them prisoner for over a year? Why should Carter have to wait for Anthony Solomon—a Federal Reserve official—to give the go-ahead before he is able to "breathe [his] sigh of relief"?

Continental Illinois: The Mega-Bailout

R ONALD REAGAN, the all-time champion free-marketeer, presided over the largest government nationalization in American history: Continental Illinois National Bank and Trust Company, in the spring and summer of 1984, a $40 billion supranational bank and the country's eighth largest before it was assaulted by an enormous worldwide run on deposits. Like many supranational banks, Continental was overextended in risky foreign loans and chancy loans to oil-exploration companies. It had made a bad portfolio worse when it purchased about $1 billion of problematic energy loans in 1982 from the failed Penn Square National Bank in Oklahoma City. Continental had to raise about $8 billion per day (half from foreign sources), called "overnight money," in order to open its doors each morning and conduct business.[68] About 40 percent of the bank's deposits were in Eurodollar accounts.[69]

When the bubble burst, Continental was hit first by large withdrawals from its Eurodollar deposits. "It's fine to fund your Eurodollar assets with Eurodollar deposits, but Continental's mistake was using Eurodollars to fund their domestic loans," the chief funding officer of another large international bank told the *Washington Post*. "The Eurodollar market is one in which concerns can get out of hand swiftly and it's difficult to get them under control quickly."[70] With domestic deposits, a bank can telephone its large institutional depositors and implore them to sit tight and not precipitate large withdrawals. Such tactics are not as effective in the impersonal supranational Eurodollar market. After the rumor mills took over, everyone joined in, and when the dust had settled an estimated $15 billion to $20 billion had been pulled out of the bank, $4 billion in one three-day period.[71] The issue facing the Reagan administration was what to do with one of the country's largest banks, whose collapse six months before a presidential election could possibly set off a chain reaction that would bring the entire financial house of cards down with it.

The solution that emerged was de facto nationalization. The Federal Deposit Insurance Corporation (FDIC), the federal agency that insures bank deposits, agreed to "purchase" between $3 billion and $4 billion of bad debts held by Continental in return for stock in the bank and the right to name a new executive team that would run the bank within a strategy devised by the FDIC.[72] That strategy called for downsizing the bank to about a $20 billion enterprise that concentrated its banking energies on regional needs instead of the supranational, high-flying business that had gotten it into trouble.

Commentators from within the banking industry lamented the demise of the supranational banking culture inside Continental that would occur through this reorganization. James Wooden of Merrill Lynch told the *Wall Street Journal* that he thought the "culture shock has to be incredible," as the reporters put it, "when low-paid FDIC regulators start calling the shots at Continental."[73] The plan to reduce Continental to a regional bank caused James D. Lowry, head of Equimark Corporation, to say: "Culturally it isn't built that way. When the mind-set has been for so many years, 'We only deal with the mega-companies and the big bucks,' you can't turn around and start saying, 'It's a great honor to lend $5 million to a guy in the machine-tool business.' "[74]

While bankers worried about Continental's pride and what might happen to the psyches of the new breed of supranational banker, the federal regulatory authorities knew they had to do more to stop the run on the bank than merely reorganize its management team. An infusion of cash of about $7.5 billion was put together to assure depositors that Continental had enough money in its vaults to cover depositors' accounts and, thereby, plug the bank's leaky financial structure. The Federal Reserve Bank of Chicago put up over $5 billion, the FDIC more than $2 billion, while twenty-eight private banks gave Continental an additional $4 billion line of credit to draw on if they needed the money.

The FDIC, in an unprecedented move, also announced that it would guarantee all deposits—even those over the $100,000 level that is their statutory obligation and is displayed on decals in the windows of banks. The treasury secretary, Donald Regan, defended the FDIC's new role as lender-of-last-resort: "We want to make sure that in these perilous times, there is no doubt that we will support our banks. That doesn't mean that every bank will remain afloat, it doesn't mean that every bank will remain independent. But nevertheless, we will make certain that there will be no calamities in the banking system."[75] The key to understanding Regan's remarks are the carefully chosen code words. What he is saying is that small banks can be permitted to fail or be taken over by another bank because they do not threaten the viability of the entire "banking system." But as the chairman of the House Banking Committee, Congressman Fernand St. Germain (D-Rhode Island), says: "The truth is that large banking institutions, despite all the talk about free enterprise, marketplaces and deregulation, do not fail under our system of government protection."[76]

Were there other options? Probably not, because the problems at Continental had been left to fester too long. The bank regulators had come to believe their own reassuring statements that they periodically issue about the soundness of the American financial system. Faced with the Continental tremor, however, and the hypothetical horror of a complete financial collapse, the Reagan administration responded by propping up the free enterprise system with massive government handouts, notwithstanding their persistent ideological defense of individual initiative and limited government intrusion into the economy. "Coercive vulnerability is the ploy the bankers use so successfully in extracting federal aid," says the financial consultant James Gipson, "providing fresh public loans to paper over dubious private ones." But the "new loans do not come cheap," he says and "the effect of the administration's rescue policy is to leave the past profits in private hands while shifting the present and future losses to the taxpayers."[77]

The real question is one of prevention. What could have been done years before the Continental disaster and what is the government doing now to forestall another banking crisis? This is a particularly important question in the light of current plans for further bank deregulation that grants the banks more leeway to do whatever they want with their depositors' money. The banking community was quick to jump on this political issue and argue that the system was sound but the banking practices of some in it imprudent: "It's not deregulation," an unnamed banking consultant told the *Wall Street Journal.* "It's idiots making stupid loans."[78]

The Political Economy of Austerity

J OHN UPDIKE, the novelist, has this fictional conversation in *The Coup* between Klipspringer, the American "financial adviser," and a Third World aspiring businessman: "The thing about indebtedness," Klipspringer says, "is it's the best insurance policy you can buy. The deeper in debt the debtor gets, the more the creditor will invest to keep him from going under. You guys were taking an incredible risk, not owing us a thing all those years."[79] This is again good advice for any individual nation but troublesome for the world as a whole if everyone follows it. And that is the predicament the world economy finds itself in today.

The Third World has accumulated debt that cannot be managed without severe austerity, absent an alternative vision of structural reform in the global economy. The United States government is running a budget deficit that sucked in about $50 billion from the rest of the world in 1984 to fund the highest federal government borrowing in its history. Banks are so overextended in their loan portfolios that the solvency of the financial system is periodically put into jeopardy. And the world's financial system is driven by unregulated supranational money, whose rapid movements cause wild exchange rate fluctuations that force governments to increase interest rates and follow policies they otherwise would not introduce.

These are the ingredients that are controlling economic policy. The actual collapse of the financial system does not have to occur; the mere threat of such a possibility is sufficient to be all consuming for policy makers. The same with Third World debt: a default does not actually have to happen, but the threat of a default is enough to structure the context in which international financial policy is developed. When such fundamentals are in place, governments have to respond to ward off the potential disasters, but the consequence of economic damage control is economic austerity.

Interest rates are the barometer of economic austerity. When the prime rate of interest rose to 13 percent in June of 1984, everyone was baffled. Nothing in the economic fundamentals could account for the run-up in the prime at that time; inflation was under control and expectations about the future were buoyant. What was missed by the pundits, however, were the political-economic milestones that had been reached in the world economy. The threat of Continental Illinois's collapse started a month earlier. The major American banks had to write off uncollected Argentine debts, and this cost them dearly in reduced profits. Chase Manhattan, for example, had its profits in the second quarter of 1984 reduced by 14 percent because of the temporary Argentine default.[80] Representatives from Latin American debtor nations were meeting in Cartagena, Colombia, to consider coordination of tactics in their debt negotiations, which raised the specter of a debtors' cartel. To compensate for losses on nonperforming loans and to hedge their bets against an uncertain future, the banks simply charged a higher rate on new performing loans. Such target return pricing is common in industry and exists in the banking world too.[81] The result is a ratcheting-up of interest rates. High interest rates and economic austerity, therefore, are endemic to the character of the post–Bretton Woods supranational economic order.

An alternative analysis exists that is based on a belief that unpredictable economic shocks—principally engineered by OPEC—sent the world economy into disarray. This school of thought would object to the analysis put forward here on two counts: first, it smacks of a conspiracy theory and, second, it is just the latest in a whole string of apocalyptic economic projections that have been proven wrong before.

It is a mistake to interpret this argument about austerity as a conspiracy theory. What is being put forward is a way of comprehending seemingly incomprehensible developments in the American economy and the world economy without resort to personality or accident. The direction that economic forces point toward is retrenchment, and that is what has been happening in the global economy since the early 1970s. Another vision could possibly extricate us from these economic forces, but short of that, the world is stuck with economic austerity as the only way to cope with the present economic predicament.

If the conspiracy charge does not stick, what of the gloom-and-doom allegation? Isn't this just an economist confirming the reputation of his profession as the dismal science? On the contrary: I have no better insight into whether the economic apocalypse will occur and if it happens, when it will hit us. What I do know, however, is that the threat of such an event is so overpowering that economic policy must dance to its rhythm. I prefer a different drummer and that is the purpose of unraveling the mystery of high interest rates and global austerity: to understand what has happened to the economy in order to provide more intelligent escape routes from the economic maze.

7

THE NEW CORPORATE
MONEY MANDARINS

T HE MEN and women who run the old, established American corporations have become primarily managers of money and only incidentally organizers of production. The engineer-manager, who worked up to the top through the ranks and was familiar with every facet of production, represents a vanishing managerial craft. Today's corporate executive has spent little time on the production floor and would be hard-pressed to name all of the holdings in the financial empire that typically bears some anonymous initials, like TRW or GTE, let alone know what is produced or how it is produced.

The corporation is seen as a locus of finance by these new money mandarins and production is what is done to justify the manipulation of money. With legal and financial backgrounds that are interchangeable among enterprises, their time span with any one company is comparatively brief. The talents of these financial administrators can be sold wherever there is a new financial war chest to manage. They gain little knowledge, therefore, of the products made in their corporate holdings before moving on to another company in an entirely different line of production to do more of the same: manage the symbols of production but never organize the actual fabrication of goods and services. The big stakes are in high finance and legal legerdemain. The psychic and financial rewards awaiting a new M.B.A. in production management are meager in contrast to what is available to an M.B.A. majoring in law or finance. Managing production has been relegated to an obsolete craft that is disappearing apace with the skilled production jobs it formerly organized.

This is a harsh indictment of the modern corporation. It originated, however, not from radical corporate-bashers but with an academic critique from the major schools of business in the United States and has been accepted by the business press and by many corporate leaders, as well. Robert B. Reich of Harvard's John F. Kennedy School of Government, calls this "paper entrepreneurialism": "generating profits through the clever manipulation of rules and numbers that only in theory represent real assets and products."[1]

This view from a social critic of the corporation was corroborated by the comment of James Roderick, chairman of U.S. Steel, when he said, "The duty of management is to make money. Our primary objective is not to make steel."[2] Roderick's background was in accounting and finance and, according to the *New York Times*, he is "less a creature of the mill than most of the top executives, having been groomed entirely on the financial side of the company."[3] Immediately after his accession to the head of U.S. Steel in 1979, Roderick abandoned plans on the drawing board to expand and modernize the company's steel-making capacity in favor of real estate ventures, the construction of a large shopping center in Pittsburgh (built with imported steel, it is rumored), and the acquisition of other companies, including paying $6 billion for Marathon Oil. Today, for the first time, a company with a proud name like United States Steel produces just about everything except steel, which accounts for less than half of the company's activities and probably will make up only a quarter of U.S. Steel's far-flung financial empire by the end of the decade.

Thoughtful members of the corporate community are concerned about the wave of mergers and acquisitions that involved nearly $350 billion between 1981 and 1984. William C. Norris, chairman of Control Data Corporation, told a Congressional committee: "In the real world, it is usually the competently managed companies that are the targets, and they are targets of firms more often driven by egos than economics."[4] And *Business Week* editorialized: "During the conglomerate drive a lot of mismatched companies found themselves floundering uncomfortably in the same corporate tent. . . . Extreme diversification diluted, and in some cases simply swamped, management abilities. In the process, a lot of fine businesses were ruined."[5]

The coincidence of the reign of money mandarins in the corporation and the development of a supranational monetary order in the banking sector is not accidental. The one feeds the other. First, the large sums of footloose cash in Eurodollar accounts need interest-bearing homes. One such home is the multi-billion-dollar loans that support mergers, almost $350 billion between 1981 and 1984. Second, the rise of finance to the commanding heights of the world economy pushed the corporation toward its own brand of financial gamesmanship at the expense of production. With the sexy, high-flying world of supranational finance as a role model, what veteran corporate executive or rookie M.B.A. could resist the temptation to replicate that world in their own company?

Third, the sharp run-up in the value of the dollar—between 33 and 50 percent against the other major currencies between 1980 and 1984—contributed to the erosion of America's industrial base. That unprecedented increase in the value of the dollar was itself a consequence of the high interest rates needed to forestall potential runs against the dollar that were due to the excessively large Eurodollar deposits. All this takes us back to the previous analysis of the development of a supranational monetary system that functioned without regulation and forced certain policy responses on sovereign governments.

An overvalued dollar hurts most those sectors that compete intensely in international markets: steel, autos, machine tools, textiles, and the like. These are the very sectors that are the sinew and muscle of an industrial economy and the ones that suffered most in the unbalanced economic recovery of the 1980s. Cities that were once the pride of the American economy—Pittsburgh, Detroit, Dayton and others of the industrial Midwest—are now turning into a rust belt. Deindustrialization is what Barry Bluestone and Bennett Harrison, professors of economics at Boston College and MIT, respectively, call this process: "widespread, systematic disinvestment in the nation's basic productive capacity . . . " where "financial resources . . . [have] been diverted from productive investment in our basic national industries into unproductive speculation, mergers and acquisitions, and foreign investment."[6]

As the number of manufacturing jobs in the old population centers shrinks, communities disintegrate and families despair. It is little comfort to an unemployed Midwest factory worker to be told about America's high-tech and service-led economic recovery of 1983–84 if its uneven effects hopscotch across industries and regions, causing booms in some and leaving busts in others. Besides, one or two years do not make a trend, and it is the trajectory of economic restructuring that is far more significant than any transitory blip. The direction of change in the American economy is toward finance and money: the rearrangement of existing real assets through the shuffling of the financial symbols of tangible wealth. The question is whether this is healthy for the American economy. Will the high-stakes financial maneuvers of the early 1980s pay off in real productive investment toward the end of the decade?

The acceleration of trends in the 1980s revealed a restructured American economy that was dependent more on financial innovations than ever before. This fact was missed by Keynesian policy makers and economists who, like their counterparts in the older manufacturing industries, continue "to take for granted, to accept as the norm of our experience, the nation's industrial growth during the first two decades after World War II."[7] The three members of the Harvard Business School who wrote this, William J. Abernathy, Kim B. Clark, and Alan M. Kantrow, go on to say that "we looked into the manufacturing accomplishments of a few remarkable years and thought we saw reflected there the whole course of our future development."[8] An economy can receive short bursts of new energy from an institutional innovation in finance such as occurred in the early 1980s. But its effects atrophy quickly and leave behind a neglected manufacturing base that may not be capable of resuscitation; witness what has happened to the British economy. "Like a prolonged high fever," warns *Business Week*, "the overvalued dollar is sapping U.S. industrial strength," raising a fear expressed by Arnold Simkin, senior economist for Merrill Lynch Economics in London, that "a share of the U.S. industrial base will be wiped out forever when this exchange rate cycle is over."[9]

Economic Restructuring in the United States

C HANGE is the norm for an economy and to say, therefore, that the American economy is undergoing an economic restructuring in the 1980s is to point blaming fingers at no one segment of society. History cannot be stopped. The reconfiguration of the economy is a fact that cannot be ignored by policy makers who should be trying to do something about the discomfort of adjustment that occurs alongside economic restructuring. In 1981, *Business Week* devoted a special report to this subject in which they said: "The American economy is undergoing a dramatic restructuring . . . in which old-line manufacturing is shrinking while energy and technology are booming . . . ," and the question is "whether the economy and the social fabric will be able to stand the strain." [10]

Trajectories of change in the U.S. economy that were apparent earlier accelerated during the supranationalization of the world economy. By the end of World War I, for example, employment in the economy was about evenly divided between service provision (transportation, trade, finance, insurance, real estate, services, and government) and goods production (manufacturing, mining, and construction). By the end of World War II, about 60 percent of employment was in service provision and 40 percent in goods production. These proportions remained fairly constant until the late 1960s, but changed rapidly during the supranational period of the 1970s. By 1980, only 28 percent of employment remained in goods production. Blue-collar production workers, who made up half of all Americans in employment after World War II, accounted for less than one-third of employment by 1980. Managerial employment, which had been steady at between 8 and 9 percent of total employment from 1900 to 1970, shot up to 11 percent in 1980, which represents a 22 percent increase in a decade.[11]

The changes in the character of employment in the U.S. economy mirror transformations in the structure of the world economy, where more industrial production is now occurring in what are called the NICs: newly industrializing countries such as Brazil, Taiwan, South Korea, and Mexico. Nowhere have the shocks to the American economic self-image been more disturbing than in the realization that the U.S. is no longer a semi-island economy, cut off from the rest of the world by two great oceans. Seventy percent of U.S. goods now compete with foreign products. Exports were nearly 20 percent of production in 1980 compared with half that amount in 1970. And imports as a proportion of domestic purchases in 1980 were over 21 percent, when they had been only 9 percent in 1970.[12] "Bred during a century of economic preeminence based on the exploitation of an internal frontier," argues *Business Week*, which more than any other business publication has devoted considerable space to these issues, "American attitudes are not suited to a world economy that has become increasingly integrated."[13]

When Bretton Woods passed from the scene in 1973, the American dollar was overvalued, but no one was prepared for the wild roller-coaster ride of the dollar over the next decade. By 1980, the dollar had fallen by about 30 percent, compared with its value in 1970. What is more disconcerting, however, is that the United States *lost* some 23 percent of its share of international markets in the 1970s at a time when a cheapened dollar should have given it a competitive advantage in world trade.[14] In the 1980s, the dollar recovered and rose by between 33 and 50 percent against most major currencies between 1980 and 1984. This has further weakened America's international trading position. If the United States could not hold on to markets when the dollar was falling, the country will not be able to reverse this trend when the rising value of the dollar makes all of its products dearer to buyers from foreign countries. The result is a trade deficit of historic proportions—$123 billion in 1984 and nearly $200 billion when 1983 is added to 1984's record trade deficit.[15]

"So high has the dollar climbed," laments *Business Week*, "that many U.S. companies find their products increasingly uncompetitive in international markets. . . . The sky-high dollar is also encouraging some companies to invest abroad rather than at home."[16] The expensive and highly valued dollar is good for tourists and American consumers who can enjoy their purchases of cheapened foreign goods but bad for people who work in sectors of the economy that are import-sensitive.

For the American business manager, contemplating whether to invest in the United States or abroad, exchange rates do matter. Unstable exchange rates make investors wary: "You don't make million-dollar investments in plant and equipment if you're unable to predict the relative exchange rates," says James A. Unruh, the chief financial officer of Burroughs Corporation.[17] A more expensive dollar induces investors to build plant and equipment in other countries at the expense of investment in the United States. As James E. Perrella, executive vice president of Ingersoll-Rand puts it: "Our responsibility in running Ingersoll-Rand is to keep ourselves competitive in world markets. . . . We are shifting our manufacturing and sourcing to countries with weaker currencies."[18]

The position of the American economy in world markets altered radically during the process of supranationalization in the 1970s. By 1981, the U.S. was importing over one-quarter of its cars, 60 percent of its consumer electronics (TVs, radios, stereos, clocks, and so on), 43 percent of its calculators, 17 percent of its steel, and 53 percent of its computerized machine tools, to cite just a few of the import proportions that affect the basic manufacturing industries that used to employ large numbers of people in stable, high-paid work.[19] For every additional $4 spent by Americans in the 1970s, $1 was for an import.[20] The auto industry, which was most affected by import penetration into what had previously been a fairly safe market for American producers, is estimated to have lost nearly half a million jobs due to auto imports by 1981, including work in direct car production and in all the industries with backward and forward linkages to the auto industry.[21]

The sum total of all these facts and figures produces a portrait of an American economy jolted from its complacent position as both the pre-eminent producer in the world economy and the unrivaled manufacturer on its own turf. While this has been happening, however, monetary power still resides unquestionably with the dollar. America's commercial position in the world economy has weakened in the 1980s, as its financial position has strengthened. This is not a terribly perplexing paradox when you contemplate for a moment what the supranational revolution of the 1970s implies: the cementing of financial bonds worldwide by a monetary network that has been able to mobilize its vast information and communications systems for the purpose of instantaneous financial transaction. The lure of this game, played on a computer screen familiar to a generation reared on Pac-man, siphons the best talent away from the gritty production pursuits that once enchanted an earlier generation of entrepreneurs brought up on Horatio Alger books.

The economies at the apex of the global system are

taking on the function of primarily servicing a supranational economic order, while ceding the mass, standardized industrial production to economies that were formerly raw-material producers on the periphery. This new international division of labor is having a profound impact on all countries, as institutions and markets lag behind in adjusting to the transformed global economic realities. At the center of this transformation is the modern multinational corporation—initially encouraged by the Bretton Woods institutions, energized by the production centers opened up by decolonization, driven to avoid high wages and government regulation at home, and now pushed to develop overseas production facilities by a strong dollar whose investment prospects are greeted with open arms by debt-poor and dollar-short Third World countries.

Between 1979 and 1984, almost a quarter of a trillion dollars was invested by U.S. firms abroad.[22] During the decade of the 1970s, when supranationalization matured, foreign investment by U.S. multinationals grew at an average annual rate of nearly 19 percent compared with only a 12 percent rate of growth of investment inside the United States on average each year.[23] The Congressional Committee on Energy and Commerce of the House of Representatives is concerned that the "difference between the process of expansion and integration of markets on the national level and the global process we are now experiencing is that the national process occurred within a single political system overseen by a sovereign federal government. . . ."[24]

No such public responsibility is exercised over the supranational economic formations, and the multinational corporation, as *Business Week* noted in 1978, is an institution whose "basic aim is to maximize worldwide profits, without regard to source of product or national boundaries. U.S. multinational managers have no business reason, therefore, for preferring to export American-made products rather than producing the same goods in foreign plants."[25] This authoritative magazine of business affairs saw no reason to change its view in 1980 when it went even further with its analysis of the modern multinational corporation:

For 25 years, U.S. companies have been participating in the global market by investing heavily overseas. . . . Aided by an overvalued dollar, U.S. corporations bought heavily into European and Third World industry. . . . The mind set of corporation executives . . . is based on selling products manufactured by plants and equipment overseas. Exporting from the U.S. is quite alien to most corporate executives, and the change in mentality itself will be traumatic.[26]

A corporate culture that values the short-term financial ploy over long-term productive investment inside the United States, while shifting its standardized manufacturing activity to other countries, poses a serious problem for employment in the American economy during the remainder of this century and beyond.

The Supranational Corporate Culture

I N CERTAIN historical periods, an identifiable corporate culture emerges that conditions the behavior, attitude, and outlook of the men and women who run the corporation. In today's supranational environment, four principles prevail: think globally, act short-term, move money, and buy and sell other corporations. Robert H. Hayes and William J. Abernathy, professors at the Harvard Business School, broke ranks with their academic colleagues when they said in

1980 that the modern corporate executive and educational institutions, like Harvard, promote a business culture that values "analytical detachment and methodological elegance over insight, based on experience, into the subtleties and complexities of strategic decisions. As a result, maximum short-term financial returns have become the overriding criteria for many companies."[27] Their influential article in the *Harvard Business Review*, "Managing Our Way to Economic Decline," that reportedly has generated more than 23,000 reprint requests, sparked a controversy in management circles that still rages today.

This preoccupation with the immediate at the expense of the future troubles many thoughtful corporate officials, among them William C. Norris, chairman of Control Data Corporation, who told a Congressional committee in 1979 that "the emphasis today is on immediate payoffs [and] in this environment, development of new products and services takes a back seat."[28] As an extension of the now generation, with an attention span more in tune with television than the patience that is required for longer-term product development, today's supranational corporate manager, in the words of David T. Kearns, president and chief operating officer of Xerox, has a "short-sighted mentality tied to the quarterly earnings report instead of the future. Risk—the very cornerstone of our capitalistic system—has become too risky."[29]

The tax system encourages this infatuation with the very short run and discourages product innovation that may take years to show positive financial results. Dividends paid out by corporations are taxed at the regular rates, but capital gains realized through the appreciation of stock values are taxed at the lower capital gains rate. A holder of stock, therefore, might prefer a short-term run-up in the value of the stock that can be cashed in and taxed at the lower capital gains rate. This has two effects: first, corporate officials will be pressed to show increases in the value of the stock—perhaps through a merger or acquisition—prompting Reginald H. Jones, retired chairman of General Electric to voice a "legitimate complaint against the tyranny of Wall Street, with its myopic concentration on reported quarterly results."[30] Second, the corporation will be encouraged by the tax system to retain earnings rather than pay them out as dividends and to use the corporate cash accumulated this way for augmentation of stock values.

To avoid the higher taxes on salaries, many corporate officials receive far more income from stock options, which are taxed at the lower capital gains rate when redeemed. This induces corporate officials to become obsessed with day-to-day stock fluctuations at the expense of longer strategic planning. "When the stock price is falling," says Reginald Jones of General Electric, "the stock options are under water, and a great deal of disaffection sets in throughout management."[31] Peter Behr of the *Washington Post* reports that 90 percent of the *Fortune* 500 have bonus payments that depend usually on earnings per share of stock.[32] "The top executives of an incredibly large number of America's best-known corporations," says Kenneth Mason, former president of Quaker Oats, "spend hundreds of man-hours a year, year after year, making sure not only that this year's annual earnings increase is consistent with last year's, but that this year's third quarter doesn't fall below last year's third quarter, or that this year's third quarter isn't so good that next year's third quarter won't be able to top it, or that this year's third quarter won't embarrass this year's fourth quarter, and so on and on."[33]

Michael Maccoby describes the dominant social character of the corporate manager as a Gamesman, interested in "competitive activity where he can prove

himself a winner."[34] Driven by what Maccoby, a psychi-
atrist, calls "fast-moving flexibility," the Gamesman is
akin to Hayes's and Abernathy's characterization of the
contemporary business leader as a "pseudo-profes-
sional"—"an individual having no special expertise in
any particular industry or technology who nevertheless
can step into an unfamiliar company and run it successfully through strict application of financial controls,
portfolio concepts, and a market-driven strategy."[35]

The financial Gamesmen start their careers in M.B.A.
programs that are bereft of courses in the management
of production. Tom Peters, co-author of the best-selling
book *In Search of Excellence*, teaches at Stanford University, whose School of Business has only two courses
on manufacturing out of ninety-one offerings, one on
sales management, and one on innovation.[36] Peters, it
should be noted, is critical of his institution for neglecting the management of production while focusing on
the creation of money managers and legal wizards. Robert B. Reich of Harvard reports that only 3 percent of the
1981 graduates of Harvard's business school took jobs
in production, compared with about 19 percent in sales
and 22 percent in finance.[37] Gerald R. Rosen, writing in
Dun's Review, cites the viewpoint of C. Jackson Grayson, president of the American Productivity Center, that
"for twenty years management coasted off the great R &
D gains made during World War II and constantly rewarded executives from the marketing, financial and
legal side of the business while it ignored the production
men." Grayson, former dean of Southern Methodist University's business school, goes on to say that "the vast
majority of today's chief executive officers did not come
up from production. Courses in the production area [in
business schools] are almost nonexistent."[38]

A 1980 study by the consulting firm Golightly and
Company reported that the top people in corporations

with legal and financial backgrounds increased by 50 percent between 1973 and 1977 from what it had been twenty years earlier, while those with technical backgrounds declined by 15 percent.[39] America now has more than 590,000 lawyers, says Robert Reich, about one for every four hundred citizens. He also points out that about two-thirds of all the members of U.S. corporate boards are trained in law, finance, or accounting, compared with Japan, where two-thirds have engineering backgrounds.[40]

W. Edward Demings, a management consultant, born at the turn of the century, who is credited with developing the Japanese management system that is the envy of the business world, says in his typically blunt manner that "populating management with financially oriented people has ruined the country."[41] Demings is somewhat of a management guru in Japan—they have even established an Oscar-type annual management prize in his name—and his view is echoed by a Japanese professor of marketing, Yoshi Tsurumi, who teaches at the Baruch College of the City University of New York: "The whole preparation of American executives tends to make them aloof from the factory floor and from the human beings who are involved in the day-to-day task of making products."[42]

Emphasis on the short-term and training in law and finance will take a manager far in a supranational monetary-driven world economy but will not make U.S. products competitive in international trade. Hayes and Abernathy sum up the problem this way: "During the past 25 years the American manager's road to the top has changed significantly. No longer does the typical career, threading sinuously up and through a corporation with stops in several functional areas, provide future top executives with intimate hands-on knowledge of the company's technologies, customers, and suppliers."[43]

As a consequence, says J. Peter Grace of W. R. Grace and Company, "he'll entertain no research, no development program that won't pay off for eight or 10 years."[44] "It's like the George Allen–type football coach," says Michael Maccoby, who originated the term "Gamesman" to describe the modern corporate official, "who trades young draft choices for 35-year-old stars who have one or two good years left. He wins immediately, but in five years he has no draft choices."[45]

Corporate management stars who hop from company to company carry with them a management philosophy that promotes the diversification of assets into what approximates a financial holding company, instead of a unified product line. Richard Rumelt of UCLA's Graduate School of Management found that after World War II, about 70 percent of the five hundred largest industrial enterprises were in a single line of business and less than 5 percent were heavily diversified. Today, less than two-fifths of the top five hundred corporations are predominantly in a single, unified line of business, while one-quarter are heavily diversified.[46]

Mergers and acquisitions are central to a corporate culture that values the big-stakes ploys that capture media headlines and position the manager to move on to another company but leave in their wake a situation, described by *Business Week*, in which "our major corporations have blossomed into multiproduct, multidivisional, multilocational hydras. They became far too diverse for any one corporate leader to embrace. So one formerly monolithic company after another decentralized into such things as profit centers, strategic business units, and the like. Every profit center had to have a general manager or a divisonal president. . . . Layer upon layer of management jobs were added to the structure."[47]

These multiheaded hydras that *Business Week* writes

about arose from a wave of mergers and acquisitions that telescoped, more than anything else, the short-term financial preoccupation of the new corporate money mandarin. To be sure, there was substantial product innovation and development in the American economy during the late 1970s and early 1980s. But most of this came from new firms in new endeavors, such as personal computers, consumer electronics, and other high-tech marvels that were not tied to the old corporate bureaucracies. The silicon valleys of America, which have become the envy of the rest of the industrial world, were not the creation of the business giants that powered the first industrial revolution but started with the new kids on the business block who saw an opportunity and seized it. The fear is that the financial war chests accumulated by the old-line companies will be used for takeovers of the new innovative enterprises that represent the best of an American entrepreneurial culture. "Like oil and water," says Arthur Burck, a consultant on corporate mergers and acquisitions, "it is difficult to mix staid bureaucracies—which by their very nature resist change—and creative, often fragile, entrepreneurial companies."[48]

In their influential 1980 article "The Reindustrialization of America," *Business Week* assesses the corporate management problem this way: "For the most part, today's corporate leaders are 'professional managers'— business mercenaries who ply their skills for a salary and bonus but rarely for a vision. . . . They become more concerned with buying and selling companies than with selling improved products to customers."[49]

Merger Mayhem

I N THE six years from 1979 to 1984, nearly $450 billion was spent in some fourteen thousand separate transactions by American corporations buying other corporations. These "recent large-scale mergers," says T. F. Russell, chairman of Federal-Mogul Corporation, "have added nothing to the economy, and may have diverted investments from areas that needed beefing up."[50] The megabuck mergers involve companies that fueled America's great industrial revolution and made it the workshop of the world: U.S. Steel bought Marathon Oil for $6 billion; du Pont bought Conoco for $7.5 billion; Standard Oil of California bought Gulf Oil for $13.5 billion; and Texaco bought Getty Oil for $10 billion. After the oil takeovers, broadcasting was next, starting with Capital Cities Communications' acquisition of ABC for $3.5 billion. Arthur Burck, the Florida consultant on mergers and takeovers, warns us that "the creation of gargantuan corporations with awesome economic and political power poses a threat to our democratic institutions," and "it is likely that by the year 2000, several score multinational corporations will control most of the nation's industrial assets. By then, our industry could be a stagnant mess, dominated by many dinosaurs."[51]

Are the tens of billions spent on mergers and acquisitions merely rearranging the deck chairs on the *Titanic*, as Burck and Russell think, or will it presage an industrial renaissance: "a more efficient corporate sector in an economy that sorely needs strengthening against a relentless foreign competition . . . leaping ahead of wrangling economists and politicians and implementing an 'industrial policy' of its own," in the words of a

1984 *Business Week* reassessment of its earlier position, which had been critical of merger mayhem.[52]

Only the passage of time will provide a definitive answer to this question, but on the evidence so far, mergers and acquisitions do not seem justified by a benefit-cost calculation. The hundreds of billions of dollars tied up in mergers and acquisitions between 1979 and 1984 is different from the investment in new plant and equipment during those same years. The tangible investment in new factories creates the foundation for jobs, while the money used for mergers and acquisitions creates no new jobs directly, except for the considerable employment of lawyers, financial consultants, and advisers in the merger business. Those who benefit most are shareholders who happen to be in the right place at the right time: "The measurable benefit of all this reordering of economic activity is mainly financial," says *Business Week*. "Shareholders are instantly rewarded as acquirers offer far more than the going market price for the shares of a company they want."[53] In fact, between 1979 and 1983, shareholders were paid an average premium of 40 percent above market price during a merger or acquisition.[54] The question is what the alternative use of $450 billion would do for the American economy— what economists call the "opportunity cost" of pursuing one activity at the expense of some other.

Perhaps the least productive use of scarce capital resources is the huge sums paid to outside consultants either to aid in the takeover battle or resist it. The tens of millions spent each year on these consultants are not even included in the $450 billion figure, which is simply the direct costs tied up in mergers and acquisitions. Morgan Stanley, for example, made nearly $15 million on the Shell Oil–Belridge Oil merger; Salomon Brothers, $6.5 million on the Elf-Acquitaine and Texasgulf deal; First Boston, a $15 million fee on the du Pont–Conoco acquisition, and so on. Pullman paid First Boston about $1,500 per hour just to resist a takeover bid.[55]

First Boston seems to have something of a corner on this market—they charged Marathon Oil $17 million in their takeover war with U.S. Steel—and their name appears alongside many of the largest consulting fees paid during mergers and acquisitions. The Wall Street firm of Kidder, Peabody & Company charges a retainer of $75,000 per year to clients on both sides of the street, those in the acquiring business and those trying to fight off acquisitions.[56] A type of protection money totaling $10 million per year is paid by some two hundred companies to the New York law firm of Skadden, Arps, Slate, Meagher & Flom, according to *Time*, "just to guarantee that [Joseph] Flom will work for them, and not against them, should they become takeover targets."[57] In 1983, about $1 billion dollars was spent on takeover consultants, topped by Getty Oil's payment to First Boston of $10 million for just seventy-nine hours of work.[58] And this tally of the unproductive use of financial and legal talent does not even take into account the waste of valuable and high-paid management time in either pursuing a takeover target or resisting a pursuer, which could be put to better use worrying about problems of production and the firm's competitive position in the world economy.

The extraordinary sums spent on consultants are due to the increase in the number of "hostile takeovers"—so-called, because the pursued would rather not have a pursuer. In the 1980s, contested takeovers were about 40 percent of the total number of acquisitions, compared with around 25 percent in the 1970s.[59] This has given rise to all manner of strategies and counterstrategies that are designed and orchestrated by the growing outside consultant business.

When William Agee, the quintessential supranational

corporate Gamesman, tried to purchase Martin Marietta for Bendix in 1982, a takeover war began that embarrassed even the most ardent participants in the conglomerate movement that has dominated the 1980s. Martin Marietta counterattacked by threatening to take over Bendix and began buying Bendix stock in what the new lexicon of merger strategies calls a "Pac-man defense." When the battlefield was exposed, United Technologies joined in and made moves to buy Bendix. In the meantime, Agee had arranged a "golden parachute"—a financial deal with his Bendix board of directors that compensated him handsomely if he had to leave Bendix after it was taken over either by United Technologies or by Martin Marietta.

Next into the fray came Allied Corporation, represented by Joseph Flom. Allied Corporation is considered a "white knight" in the new glossary of terms that has grown up in the past ten years around corporate takeovers: "a company enlisted to take over a concern that is trying to escape a less desirable takeover."[60] A total of $5.6 billion in lines of credit to the four companies was provided by twenty-eight major U.S. banks and eleven foreign banks, prompting Henry S. Reuss (at the time a Democratic congressman from Wisconsin and chairman of the Joint Economic Committee) to say: "Millions of ordinary Americans are not amused by this spectacular misuse of their savings by the corporate world and the banking system."[61]

When the dust had settled, United Technologies dropped out of the battle, and a deal was struck that permitted Allied Corporation to take over Martin Marietta, along with a stock swap that involved Bendix giving Allied its stock in Martin Marietta in exchange for the Bendix stock that Martin Marietta had bought during its Pac-man defense. The tragedy is that three strong companies became three weaker companies after the takeover war. A report in the *Washington Post* in early 1983, about three months after the takeover encounter, revealed that Martin Marietta had to sell off its profitable cement division for $300 million in order to raise the money it needed to service the $900 million debt it had accumulated to defend itself against the Bendix acquisition that it never wanted or encouraged in the first place.[62]

Arthur Burck, himself a merger and acquisition consultant, is concerned that "this buy-ruin-and-sell process has already undermined a generation of the country's most promising enterprises."[63] Martin Marietta was not alone in finding itself short of cash to both run a company and pay off the enormous debts accumulated during a takeover battle. To buy Conoco, du Pont's debt more than tripled to $3.9 billion, requiring annual payments of about $600 million. Fluor Corporation had to sell off $174 million of the assets of St. Joe Minerals (which it had just acquired) to reduce the debt it had incurred during the takeover of St. Joe's.[64]

The ultimate in corporate cannibalization is a strategy known variously as either "scorched earth" or "selling off the crown jewels": a company being pursued in a hostile takeover sells off its most valuable assets in order to reduce its attractiveness to the pursuer. And then there is the "greenmail" strategy, used by Saul Steinberg in his fray with Walt Disney Productions. Here, a corporate raider buys a toehold position and threatens a takeover bid. In subsequent negotiations, the pursuer agrees to sell back the stock at an above-market price in return for abandoning the takeover attack. In the case of Steinberg and Disney, he bought 11 percent of Disney stock and then sold it back to the company above market for $325.3 million. After Steinberg pulled out, Disney stock tumbled, burning all those investors who came in behind Steinberg, thinking they would make a killing on the acquisition battle as others had done in different takeovers.[65]

Sometimes it is hard to know where the video games played in amusement centers end and business reality begins. Does corporate life imitate the video game or the game corporate life? Whatever, the stakes are significant and the waste prolific, as money, time, and talent are diverted from the real job of producing a competitive product that can hold its own in the world economy. William Norris, in Congressional testimony, said that "immediately after a takeover, an innovation-stifling process sets in. The aggressor blankets the other with bureaucracy, layer upon layer. Proposals for new products languish. The result is the dispersal of the entrepreneurial team, the major job-creating resource."[66]

The Eurodollars Come Home to Roost

T HE POWER of Eurodollars and the supranational monetary system reveals itself in the way it has influenced the development of a new corporate culture in America. A short-term financial orientation in the corporation is ideally suited to a world of supranational money that constantly needs to find lucrative interest-bearing places to invest the hundreds of billions that make up the Eurodollar system. For about a decade, up to 1983, the Third World absorbed the bulk of Eurodollar lending. When that turned sour, after Mexico, Argentina, and Brazil could not pay back their debts without massive reschedulings, the supranational banks pulled back from additional large-scale lending to the less-developed countries. By the mid-1980s, Eurodollar lending to the Third World was only a small fraction of what it was before, apart from the sums used to reschedule debts and prop up countries so they could maintain the fiction of solvency. Enough money was lent out to pay back past interest, so the banks' profits and balance sheets could continue to look respectable. The principal on the loans due, however, was not repaid but was simply reformulated into new debts. The question for the supranational banks, therefore, was where would the Eurodollars go when the major source of Third World borrowing dried up?

One such place was to American corporations that borrowed short-term in wholesale amounts to finance the billions needed for raids on other companies. In the process, however, tendencies that were developing in the American corporate culture became exaggerated. A short-term financial preoccupation in the corporation intersected with the supranational banking world's need to find a new home for its footloose Eurodollars. The hot money moving around the world found a fresh place to roost. Conveniently, the Reagan administration removed any antitrust threats that may have inhibited corporations from buying up each other. They even stopped collecting statistics on mergers and acquisitions, as if to say: hear no evil, see no evil . . .

Still on the drawing board, but destined to play a large role in Eurodollar lending by the end of the 1980s, are plans for so-called megaprojects: a Channel tunnel that will link France and Great Britain, known as the Chunnel project, and a bridge-tunnel link between Sweden and the Continent, the Scanlink. Coupled with these two projects, which would connect all of Europe and Great Britain, is a scheme to build high-speed roads and rail systems that will enable someone to drive from London to Oslo in ten hours, without ever using a ferry, or speed from Manchester in the north of England to Milan on a train in five or six hours. The Roundtable of European Industrialists, an elite discussion group of twenty-two leading European industrialists that is sponsoring these ideas, estimates the costs in the tens of billions, with financing from the Eurodollar markets and some government backup. Adrian Hamilton, the industrial editor of the British newspaper the *Observer*, says that the banks see in these projects "politically safe opportunities for large scale financing after the horrors of Third World debt and energy project disasters."[67]

A third comfortable nesting place for Eurodollars is the borrowing by the U.S. government to finance its large and growing budget deficits—about $600 billion between 1981 and 1984. U.S. government borrowing is perfectly compatible with a new supranational monetary order that wants to lend its Eurodollars on a short-term wholesale basis in relatively secure places. And the high real rates of interest paid by the U.S. Treasury provide the banks with a handsome profit. This explains how the U.S. government can run up its budget deficit to close to $200 billion per year, and borrow in financial markets, without undue stress on interest rates or without crowding out private borrowing. The oft-predicted sharp rise in interest rates as a result of increased government borrowing has not happened because of the Eurodollar safety valve. The pundits who offer these predictions neglect to take into account the fact that the potential borrowing reach of the government extends beyond the narrow definition of lendable funds within the fifty states. They have failed to acknowledge or grasp the significance of the new supranational monetary system in all its dimensions, including the need for a new statistical definition of the money supply and lendable funds.

Since the biggest increase in federal expenditures has been for military hardware, the real effect of Treasury borrowing is to place the national government in the role of a financial intermediary for the defense industry. Government borrows from private financial markets— and increasingly from Eurodollar markets—then passes that money through to defense contractors. In one door comes the supranational money and out the other it goes to the defense industry to fund America's version of megaprojects. Defense contractors can then leverage their government orders into additional borrowing from the private financial markets.

It is a neat system that would cause howls of protest were it applied to any other sector of the American economy, such as education or an industrial policy for civilian manufacturing. It is aided and abetted by a supranational monetary system that permits large-scale government borrowing without hitting interest rate ceilings or crowding out the private sector from borrowing in financial markets. So well camouflaged are the workings of this arrangement that nothing is exposed to a public debate that recognizes the trade-off between using the government's borrowing from the supranational monetary system for defense as opposed to a similar arrangement in another sector of the American economy.

8

WHAT'S LEFT?
POLITICAL ECONOMY IN
THE SUPRANATIONAL ERA

OLITICS in America is held captive by political-economic mythologies that distort economic history and pre-empt serious debate about economic problems. The conservative mythology sees the country's economic history in terms of how the West was won: by a rugged individualism that brought prosperity to an untamed land. This was accomplished, the story goes, without government assistance, by pushing the harsh frontiers outward, and through a belief that all was possible if only people were free to follow their self-interest and natural talents. Technology tamed the environment and enabled deserts to blossom into agricultural cornucopias. Cities challenged nature by standing on earthquake faults, and business ingenuity provided the coolant that made life possible in 100-degree heat. The sons and daughters of these pioneers now do battle against another foe: the government, which they "speak of," says Robert Heil-

broner, "as if it were a foreign power occupying the nation's capital," standing in the way of everything their
America stands for.[1]

The liberal mythology is about how the country, east
of the Mississippi, was won by Italian grocers, Jewish
tailors, Irish policemen, Scandinavian farmers, Slavic
steelworkers, and Hungarian coal miners. Their story is
about how a beneficent government opened the door to
the American dream for their children. Some of the sons
and daughters of these immigrants, however, have
traded the union cards of their parents for engraved
invitations to white-wine-and-Brie receptions. Yuppies,
they are called, and the old liberal politics of their fore-
bears does not speak to their aspirations. To them, liberals are peering through political lenses that were
ground in the 1930s, improved in the 1960s, but are in
need of refraction in the 1980s.

Nineteen eighty-four was a pivotal year in which the
two mythologies clashed in the presidential election. A
new conservatism has established firm roots, and whatever happens in the next presidential election, it is here
to stay. "Mr. Reagan," says the *Economist*, "has introduced a new politics, which uneasily yokes a radical,
forward faith in the virtue of change with true, back-
ward-looking conservatism."[2] An early-nineteenth-cen-
tury free-market parable about multitudes of small
producers, competing for the dollars of all-powerful consumers, is being used by the new conservatives as a
modernizing ideology in a late-twentieth-century environment of supranational financial behemoths.

Liberal politics and Keynesian economics have been
overtaken by this revolution in ideas that replaced a
consensus that had reigned for nearly half a century. No
longer is government seen as the ally of economic progress; the private market has been resurrected as an engine of economic change that will operate effectively,

according to the new conservatives, if only government would leave it alone. "Americans have become readier than at any time since the 1930s to let their economic development be decided by what a free market . . . happens to turn up," says the *Economist* in its 1984 retrospective.[3]

The ideological insurrection, effectively mounted by new conservatives from the West and South against liberals from the East and Northwest, is called supply-side economics. This doctrine asserts that wealthy people have their incentives to work hard in the economy diminished by an after-tax income that is too *low*, whereas working people have their incentives diminished by an after-tax income that is too *high*. Tax cuts, skewed toward the upper reaches of the income distribution, coupled with wage restraints and an assault on the public undergirdings to the private wage, make up the programmatic implementation of supply-side philosphy. Nothwithstanding David Stockman's admission that supply-side doctrine was "always a Trojan horse to bring the top [tax] rate down," the idea has gained a political currency that is similar to the acceptance of the Keynesian revolution twenty years ago.[4] Both appeared to deliver on their promises of economic renewal.

More can be made of the differences between conservative supply-side and Keynesian demand-side economic policy than is warranted, however. Both depend on fiscal stimulus to generate economic growth through a combination of tax cuts and/or spending increases. The Reagan administration has done both and, therefore, many economists would argue, has simply confirmed the Keynesian nostrums.

The emergence of a new conservatism coincided with the rise of a supranational economic order, not just in the United States, but in most of the other industrial democracies as well. The two developments are more than a coincidence. The supranational economy functions with fewer public controls than has heretofore been the norm. This is particularly true of the monetary sector, where the deregulation of international money between the years 1971 and 1973 created a vacuum that was filled by private international banking and by Euro-dollars that operated as a form of private, stateless money outside the jurisdiction of national governments. In this international environment, the catchwords of the new conservative national ideology became acceptable: deregulation, free enterprise, and privatization.

Government's problem, in this supranational environment, is to try to control money and its value. This preoccupation supplants policy makers, concerned with employment and growth, with money mandarins whose primary objective is to restrain economies so that the value of money is kept reasonably stable. The employment- and growth-oriented policy makers tend, on average, to be Keynesian in their economics and to tilt toward liberalism in their politics. Money mandarins incline toward conservative politics and monetarist economics.

This way of looking at the political transformation of the 1980s contrasts with the current fashion, which is to locate the source of change in the crisis of the welfare state. In this formulation, the expansion of social welfare programs, and the government's success in reducing economic insecurity, so demoralized the private sector of the economy that incentives for economic growth were undermined. It stands to reason, therefore, if this analysis is accepted, that a restoration of the private impetus for growth requires a reimposition of economic insecurity by reducing government's ability to make economic life for its citizens more secure. It is the nervous energy thrown forth by insecurity that promotes economic growth, according to this view. Setting aside the dubious psychological basis and moral implications of this theory, its analytical premise is also open to question.

A more cosmic set of supranational forces has swept over the world's economies and left them with an inability to grow fast enough to support the public's expectation for more economic security from their government. Rather than the crisis of the welfare state causing inadequate growth, supranationalism promotes a global austerity that leads to government's inability to fund the growing claims on the welfare state. The public complaint, therefore, is misplaced. It is directed at government and not at unregulated supranationalism. Until this debate is clarified, political discourse will continue to be about mythologies, and electoral victory will go to the best storyteller.

As supranationalism weakens the government's ability to manage its economy, the argument that government should step aside and turn over all responsibility to private markets seems more valid. This is precisely what happened in the decade after the end of Bretton Woods. Governments abdicated their public responsibility over international money, and this produced a largely unmanageable world economy, where private actors played the lead roles and governments had the bit parts. The supranational process erodes the public's role in economics and creates the very self-fulfilling prophesy that permits a free-market ideology to gain currency. The key, therefore, to reasserting a balance between private pursuits and the public good is to restore some semblance of governance over the world economy in order to reduce the influence of private supranational forces. Only then can the idea of a genuinely mixed economy, which represents all segments of society, achieve the legitimacy it needs to initiate a political dialogue that is rooted in the realities of the last fifth of the twentieth century.

Welfare: Individual and General

F OR SOME two hundred years," says Vermont Royster of the *Wall Street Journal*, "we've debated what the phrase 'general welfare' implies. For some it means a government that stands aloof, or at least governs least, creating a climate in which each citizen is left free to provide for his own welfare. For others it means a government that supports a welfare state. . . ."[5] A resurgent free-market conservatism has redefined politics in the 1980s and convinced the public that a government that governs *selectively,* rather than least, is the one that can best promote individual economic rights. In retreat is a twentieth-century liberalism that argues it promotes individual economic rights most effectively by using government to provide both the economic opportunity and security that a free market, left alone, cannot offer.

Consider the board game Monopoly: the game is played by first distributing money equally at the start. The throw of the dice determines who makes the first move. These are both theoretical ideals—perfect equality and chance—which cannot be replicated in society but are implicit in the free-market, textbook model on which conservatives base their beliefs. The game is played out; one person wins, the others lose. The losers say: "Let's play another game. Throw all our money and property back into the common pot, and we will distribute income equally again." "Wait," says the winner. "I accumulated my income and property by the strength of my own wits. I will not be expropriated. Let's play the game from where the last one ended and see who wins the next one." The outcome would be obvious, and the losers would never play the game under these circumstances. The free-market game of life, however, is closer to the "conservative" monopoly rules described here than it is to the rules on the game's box.

The debate over economic philosophy between conservatives and liberals revolves around the extent to which the government should act as rule maker and intervene to protect individual economic rights. Conservatives would circumscribe such intervention, leaving the problem of individual economic rights solely to the free market, while liberals reject the idea that a free market alone can effectively protect economic rights. Recognizing the importance and efficiency of the market in regulating the economy, liberals contend, however, that government is needed as a referee to supplement the market when it comes to questions of individual economic rights. On the other hand, conservatives maintain that, by intruding on the market's jurisdiction, the government will inevitably reduce the market's ability to allocate resources efficiently and regulate the economy effectively. The result will be slow growth, economic inefficiency, and a demoralized economy conservatives, like Mancur Olson, fear: "An economy with free markets and no government or cartel intervention is like a teenaged youth; it makes a lot of mistakes but nonetheless grows rapidly without special effort or encouragement."[6]

Around this core debate over how best to promote individual and general welfare, there is a cycle in the public's infatuation with one or the other economic philosophy. In the mid-to-late nineteenth century, the free-market position was dominant, supplanted in the middle of the twentieth century by a liberalism that was identified with the goals of economic equity, social justice, and using the government as mediator between the individual and market outcomes. It pursued economic equity and social justice by advocating policies that promoted economic security and equality of opportunity. In both areas, the government was given new roles and expanded authority compared with its functions in the nineteenth century. An intellectual revolution, which began at the turn of the century, started to take shape after World War I. It found a new urgency during the Great Depression, became the governing philosophy after World War II, and dominated public policy until the conservative counterrevolution of the 1980s.

The High-Wage Economy

A LONGSIDE these shifts in political ideas, there was an upheaval in political-economic thought that started in Great Britain at the turn of the century with the work of economists who were also social reformers. The most famous of these, Sidney and Beatrice Webb, were members of the Fabian Society, an association of intellectuals, writers, and political activists. The society was founded in 1885, and its work formed the intellectual backbone of the British Labour party up to the 1980s.

Beatrice Potter Webb was the daughter of a successful Gloucester businessman. She took up the plight of workers and the poor in Victorian England, first by working with her cousin, Charles Booth, on what became a classic in social research: *The Life and Labour of the People in London.* In 1891, she published her own study, *The Co-operative Movement in Great Britain,* which stands today as a basic reference work on alternative forms of economic organization. She met Sidney Webb in 1890, and they were married in 1892, forming a partnership that dominated British intellectual life on the left through World War I. They founded the London School of Economics, were instrumental in educational reform in Great Britain, and drafted the Labour party's policy statement in 1918, *Labour and the New Social Order,* which was the first of several documents that guided the party through its programmatic reforms after World War II. It was the Webbs who first set down on paper the fundamentals of the welfare state. Their most famous works were two volumes on the British labor movement: *The History of Trade Unionism* and *Industrial Democracy.*

In those books are the ideas for a way of looking at an economy that stood traditional economics on its head. A high-wage economy, they argued, would not be detrimental to growth and efficiency, as the conventional wisdom of their day and ours believes. Rather an economy of high wages can be viewed as supportive of the very objectives for which traditional, free-market economics claims a monopoly: economic growth and efficiency. The high wages and improved working conditions sought by trade unions have two salutary effects on the economy, according to the Webbs, beyond the individual benefits for the workers receiving them. First, the high-wage economy improves overall efficiency in the system by weeding out the least-productive firms, leaving only those companies in business that are capable of paying high wages, while continuing to earn sufficient profits. Therefore, the productivity of the economy as a whole is enhanced, and this leads to higher economic growth, the basis for improved standards of living. This is a form of economic Darwinism, to be sure, put forward during a period when Darwin and his ideas were very influential. Those workers displaced by the survival-of-the-fittest effect of high wages would find work through a governmental commitment to employment objectives, also advocated by the Webbs.

The second positive effect of high wages is in the increased consumer purchasing power that stimulates economic activity by providing the markets for goods and services. This became a cornerstone of Keynes's work during the Great Depression. His construction of a theory and policies, to achieve full employment through government monetary and fiscal measures, provided the practical means of realizing the Webbs' employment objectives.

The economic growth, created through the high-wage economy, provides the social dividends that finance the welfare state and pay for greater economic security: unemployment compensation, Social Security, Medicare, and the rest of the programs that make up modern social policy. "The quest for prosperity," says the economic journalist Robert J. Samuelson, "engaged a twin promise: a constant rise in living standards and an escape from insecurity. This concept of progress pervaded postwar politics and institutional development. It motivated the modern welfare state and oriented government policy toward constant economic growth."[7]

The high-wage economy attracted support after World War II, because it seemed to be replete with benefits for all, what today would be called a positive-sum game. Growth would be created by the high rates of increase in labor productivity. Aggregate demand and high levels of employment would be sustained by consumer purchasing power. If public policy was committed to full employment, fiscal and monetary management would complement the high-wage economy to ensure the optimum social welfare. As if to underscore the United States' acceptance of these ideas, the Employment Act of 1946 enshrined into law the government's responsibility to pursue policies that would produce high levels of employment.

There were, of course, rough edges around this core consensus. In the United States, discrimination against black workers revealed a contradiction in the model when the civil rights movement of the 1950s and 1960s erupted. A decade later, the same discrepancy was pointed out by the women's movement. General conditions of poverty in the society showed that not all workers received high wages and challenged America's self-identity as an affluent society. An income distribution that remained unaltered after World War II conflicted with the American dream of social mobility. But these problems were merely chinks in the armor of the core consensus and could be contained within it, at least according to the proponents of the model of a high-wage economy. The Great Society took on the problems of those groups left out of the high-wage economy. Fiscal and monetary policies provided the aggregate Keynesian context for the specific Great Society programs that were targeted to reach those people ignored by the high-wage economy.

This notion of a high-wage economy, augmented by the Great Society, has a certain soothing logic to it. The question is: where did it go wrong? Was it because government overstepped the bounds and began to introduce policies that inhibited growth, the conservative view; or was it because external shocks—like OPEC—reduced growth and soured the country on its welfare commitments, the mainstream liberal view? There is another explanation, however, located in the character of a supranational economy, which involves the with-holding of productive investment from the economy by private enterprise.

The Strike of Capital

T HE ONE problem, more than any other, that has caused the liberal high-wage project to founder is its inability to integrate private capital into its program without precipitating a withdrawal of in-vestment from the economy by private wealth holders. The proclivity of private capital to go on strike when it faces a situation not to its liking creates a problem for the high-wage economy that has ecsaped a solution up to now. A strike of capital is a powerful form of passive resistance that can thwart the goals of liberal social de-mocracy. No conspiracy is needed to do this; all the pri-vate owner has to do is follow his profit-maximizing instincts. And if enough do it, the economy can come to a screeching halt when capital goes on strike. While there are laws pertaining to strikes of labor, there are none that address the corollary strike of capital. Property law, in this sense, has not caught up with the institutional reality of a late-twentieth-century supra-national economy, dominated by large private enter-prises that can easily escape the discipline of a textbook, free-market economy. Liberalism has found no way to confront this problem effectively, and consequently, it has begun to falter and show signs of retreat from its objectives.

A strike of capital, like a strike of labor, is simply the withholding of a factor of production from the process of producing commodities and providing services. As a result, less is produced than would otherwise be the case. It exists because there are alternative ways to earn a return on capital that do not involve production. The owner of private capital can simply refuse to reinvest in an existing productive apparatus and instead put all the financial resources into paper assets. Today, there has been a proliferation of such paper assets, and they have grown considerably over the past decade. This represents hoarding: the complete withholding of financial resources from productive use and their transformation into paper assets. The value of these paper assets can increase due to short-term speculation and long-term increases in the demand for them, as more wealth holders move their assets out of production and into paper.

The extraordinary growth in mergers and acquisitions is a second way in which capital can be withheld from productive investment. Such activities create no new productive assets but simply rearrange existing wealth among different owners, while sequestering vast sums of money that could be used productively to create growth and employment.

In the United States, where some public regulation of capital is an individual state function, the private investor can move productive assets from one part of the country to another. This is a selective strike of capital, because it is applied to just one section of the country. For example, states in the sunbelt, with a more restrictive stance toward unions and easier pollution laws, have been the beneficiaries of investment at the expense of the frostbelt states that take a tougher policy line on pollution and are more supportive of trade union organization. In this way, federalism has enabled a selective strike of capital to occur.

The corporation can take a bolder step and move an entire factory to another country. The multinational corporation, with its ability to move plants from one nation to another, has rewritten the production rule book in the world economy. Here, the strike of capital is not applied selectively within a country but takes the form of capital flight that can affect the entire nation.

Whichever of these four devices of capital strike are used—hoarding, mergers and acquisitions, selective strike, or capital flight—the results are similar in their impact on liberal social democracy. Capital has been able to escape liberalism's reach and, by so doing, weakens the entire welfare state enterprise. The government sees its long-term strategy and specific public policies eroded by the responses of capital.

The supranational system facilitates capital strikes. The proliferation of paper assets is a feature of the supranational economy, and this encourages hoarding. The growth of mergers and acquisitions is fed by a supranational corporate culture that provides the managerial rationale, while the Eurodollars provide the wherewithal, for multi-billion-dollar rearrangements of existing assets. The multinational corporate process has been energized by a supranational monetary system that provides ready access to billions of dollars for investment in other countries at relatively lower rates of interest than would be paid inside the United States.

Supranationalism breaks down the public's role in an economy and permits private economic forces to trade economic and social policies across national borders. Capital has become mobile on a worldwide basis, while labor remains confined, for the most part, to a specific country. This discordance between the international extension of capital and the national confinement of labor has weakened labor's political role in the supranational era and added to the decline of liberalism as a governing program.

The new conservative movement, however, has had

little difficulty in fashioning a public policy agenda that responds to the problem of capital being withheld from productive use. It proposes a restoration of financial incentives so that private capital will return to productive investment. The mechanism by which this is accomplished harkens back to conservative first principles: rely upon the market, with limited government intrusion. Taxes, regulatory policy, antitrust law, and whatever stands in the way of capital coming off strike should be recast in order to encourage private initiative.

Supranationalism and the new conservatism, therefore, march down the same path, while liberalism has not yet come to grips with this new worldwide phenomenon. In this arena, liberalism is also at odds with the country's long-standing belief in the free market. While private enterprise enjoys a solid legitimacy in America, the government's role in providing economic security and opportunity is comparatively new and its root structures are not strong enough to withstand the forces that threaten to tear them up.

The Two Cultures: Political and Economic

W E LIVE in a world that is at once both political and economic. The market has never been separable from politics, no matter what free-market utopians say, because the one cannot be dissociated from the other. Questions that appear to be purely political invariably have a hidden economic substance to them. This connection between politics and economics —political economy—is sharpened in the supranational era. The IMF has politicized many issues that previously were shrouded in technical economic language. Exchange rates carry with them political implications for the governments of the day in the countries that are buffeted by their ups and downs. The link between a supranational monetary order and financial solvency has interjected the political process into private banking affairs on an unprecedented scale, as in the case of Continental Illinois or any of several dozen Third World countries. And the political edge of monetarism is difficult to conceal from those who are adversely affected by its economic consequences.

While politics is inextricably entangled with economics, and vice versa, the two systems are based on distinctly different premises. Therein lies much of the conflict between liberalism and conservatism, as well as much of the confusion surrounding the contemporary debate over economic policy.

In all the industrial democracies, the cultural values of the political and economic systems are in conflict. The political system is organized formally on the principle of "simple equality," a term used by the political philosopher Michael Walzer: one person, one vote, which is achieved through universal suffrage.[8] Of course, simple equality does not exist in fact, because some people have more informal political power than others. However, what is important for the legitimacy of the political system is not the actual existence of simple equality, but a belief in this principle as an ideological underpinning of the political system.

The economic system, by way of contrast, is based on *inequality:* one dollar, one vote. Some degree of inequality is accepted as necessary in the economic system to provide the private incentives that motivate people to energize the economy. There is an inherent tension, therefore, between the values of these two systems, in the sociologist Daniel Bell's terminology: a "cultural contradiction" of capitalism.[9]

Nowhere is this contradiction more apparent than in

the international institutions created after World War II. The political institutions enshrined in the United Nations are based on the principle of one nation, one vote, with the exception of the Security Council. The economic institutions created at Bretton Woods, however, are based on the principle of one dollar, one vote. Voting power in the IMF and World Bank is based on a formula that depends on the financial endowments put up by its member governments. About eight countries have half the votes; the United States share of the total vote is about one-fifth. Politics was formally split from economics in the postwar international institutions, but the day-to-day reality of nation-state relations makes no such artificial distinction.

Part of the conflict between Third World countries and industrial nations can be understood in this context. The developing countries prefer to take their economic grievances to the political process at the United Nations, and the industrial countries defer to the Bretton Woods economic institutions. The reasons are obvious: in the political forum, based on one nation, one vote, the more-numerous LDCs have greater power, while in the one-dollar, one-vote economic institutions, the voting power is in the hands of the industrial countries. The Third World charges the industrial countries with being undemocratic by relying on institutions where voting power is weighted by capital subscriptions. The industrial countries charge the LDCs with seeking to politicize economic questions, and submit them to "simple equality," when these economic issues are more narrowly technical in nature and not amenable to a one-nation, one-vote principle. Truth and justice do not necessarily reside with either side. All that is happening in this dispute is a preference by the two sides for either a political or an economic culture, depending on which is more suitable for their specific objectives.

This division between the economic and political cultures in the postwar international institutions can be seen in their origins. The meetings that led to the United Nations took place in San Francisco, while the meetings about the postwar economic institutions were on the other coast at Bretton Woods. The Treasury took the lead role at Bretton Woods, and the State Department performed this function at the UN meetings. This split in authority exists to this day, with Treasury in control at the World Bank and IMF and State at the UN.

The value systems of the economic and political cultures coexist, but do so in an unstable truce. The political system cannot function without a commitment to formal equality. On the other hand, left to its own devices, the free-market economic system tends to generate inequalities that the political system cannot ratify without threatening its own legitimacy, based on formal voting equality. Social welfare policies are a way in which the political system inserts its ideological commitment to formal equality into an economic system, which needs to sustain inequalities in order to defend the private incentives that motivate the economy.

The tension between these two powerful competing institutions establishes the conditions for pendulum-like swings in public support for social welfare policies. They represent the political system's affirmation of its ideological values over those of the economic system. The degree of support for social welfare policies and liberalism, therefore, is an indication of the relative influence of the political culture over the economic culture. In the late 1970s and early 1980s, as the supranational system matured, the pendulum swung toward the value structure of the economic system.

The supranational economy, by definition, erodes the importance of the economic role of the nation-state while elevating the influence of private economic values. As the economic functions of the nation-state are weakened in the supranational era, the political system cannot advocate its values of equality as effectively as before. The result is a retreat from social welfare policies, an assertion of economic values over political values, and a privatization of what had previously been public obligations.

Individual and Group Claims

MUCH IS made today about how the excessive claims on government budgets by special-interest groups have undermined the growth potential of the American economy. William Greider, who received David Stockman's confession during his early days as head of President Ronald Reagan's Office of Management and Budget, says that Stockman thought "liberal politics in its later stages had lost the ability to judge claims, and so yielded to all of them . . . ," precluding the liberals from addressing "larger national interests."[10] In a recent book that has become very influential in new conservative circles, Mancur Olson weaves an entire theory about the rise and fall of nations around the growth of interest groups, which he calls "distributional coalitions." According to Olson, these distributional coalitions pursue "collective action within societies [that] are . . . overwhelmingly oriented to struggles over the distribution of income and wealth . . . in ways that reduce social efficiency and output."[11]

This way of looking at interest-group politics stands pluralism on its head—a doctrine that used to be celebrated as a chief virtue of American politics. And it is not confined to new conservatives. John W. Gardner, founder of Common Cause and President Lyndon Johnson's secretary of health, education and welfare, has written: "Each has achieved veto power over a piece of any possible solution, and no one has the power to solve the problem. Thus in an oddly self-destructive conflict, the parts wage war against the whole," and this is the "central problem of pluralism today."[12] Negative power is exercised by interest groups within a pluralistic system according to the liberal formulation of the problem, and there is no clear mechanism that can extricate the political system from gridlock. "Economic liberalism," says the liberal social critic Fred Hirsch, "is in this sense a victim of its own propaganda: offered to all, it has evoked demands and pressures that cannot be contained."[13]

The interest groups, derided by both conservatives and liberals, represent a form of group claim on the economy's output that is articulated through the political process. These are of a different species from the individual claims made on the market economy. Individual claims, such as wages and salaries or profit, are consistent with the view of a market as a place where meritocracy rules, and the incomes received are the just rewards for work. Group claims, on the other hand, are seen as undermining the market process that permits individual claims to be exercised.

This legitimacy gap exists because individual claims on the market are compatible with America's primary symbols, while group claims rely upon the use of the political culture, which is seen as transgressing its jurisdiction when it tries to adjudicate economic claims. While "ours is an age of group consciousness," says the economist Lester Thurow, "the whole concept of group, as opposed to individual, justice is one that Western societies find difficult to handle. . . . The Western tradition is one of justice for individuals and not social justice for groups."[14]

This places liberalism in a particularly awkward corner. Group claims, and the use of the political system's cultural values in economic affairs, each lack a support language and a historical tradition. When the two are combined, the delegitimation is compounded. The question that needs to be asked, however, is why do individual claims on the market receive such acclaim, while group claims in the political system lack the ideological foundation to sustain them when the economy's growth rate falters?

Programmatic Liberals and Ideological Conservatives

AMERICANS have a split personality about politics. Opinion surveys for the past two decades show that they support specific liberal programs, combined with an abstract conservative ideology that is at odds with their support for programmatic liberalism. When asked in the mid-1970s, for example, by Everett C. Ladd, Jr., a political scientist who specializes in political attitude research, whether the federal government was too strong, 72 percent of those surveyed said yes. And 83 percent thought the federal government spent too much money. At the same time, Ladd found the identical respondents favoring a national health insurance program (67 percent) and more spending for education (89 percent).[15]

In the 1980s, with the Reagan revolution at full steam, opinion surveys still showed broad public support for the liberal programs most under attack—Social Security, business regulation, and pollution controls. A

Harris poll, for instance, found that 60 percent of Americans wanted a tougher Clean Water Act in 1983, compared with 45 percent in 1981, when Reagan took office; about 47 percent favored a stricter Clean Air Act in 1983, versus 29 percent in 1981.[16]

Nearly two decades earlier, at the height of the Great Society in the mid-1960s, when one would have expected a different set of public attitudes, two political scientists, Lloyd A. Free and Hadley Cantril, discovered a pattern of political beliefs much like today. They found that about two-thirds of their respondents were "operational liberals" in their support for specific New Deal and Great Society programs. On the other hand, they classified about one-half of their respondents as ideological conservatives, based on a series of questions about the role of government in society, individualism, and government regulation of business. "This discrepancy between operational outlooks and ideological views," they say, "is so marked as to be almost schizoid."[17] Free and Cantril identified 23 percent of the American population as holding political beliefs that were both ideologically conservative and programmatically liberal at the same time.[18] It is interesting to note that this figure, roughly one-fourth, is about the same as the typical undecided vote before an election. No doubt this swing group, made up of conflicting attachments, has difficulty making up its mind on whether to vote its ideological or programmatic inclinations.

The more local the election, the more the electorate decides on programs. At the national level, however, there is a stronger tendency for the electorate to want to make a statement about what America stands for. Here ideology, mythology, and storytelling about America is more important than the administrative alphabet that preoccupies bureaucratic Washington. Conservatives have done well at the presidential level since Roosevelt, because they have developed a more convincing story about America that identifies with the voters' instincts. Liberals have done better at lower levels—the cities, state legislatures, and governorships—where programs matter more than ideology. This explains why the House of Representatives has always been more predominantly Democrat-controlled than the Senate, where more of the electorate wants to make its ideological comment on America. Particularly in an age dominated by television, the electorate does not want to put someone in the White House who would broadcast the wrong story about America.

Liberals currently lack an attractive political mythology to complement the public acceptance of their programs, while conservatives have thin support for their programs but considerable ideological identification with American political beliefs. The liberal task, therefore, is to explain their program in a way that touches an ideological nerve in the public. The conservative's is to fashion programs that are acceptable to American attitudes about their government. Whichever group can close the gap between ideological and program support will produce the dominant governing philosophy for many years. If neither conservatives nor liberals are successful at this, politics will continue to swing back and forth like a pendulum, depending on whether the electorate vote their ideological or programmatic beliefs. This accounts for Albert Hirschman's observation that "Western societies appear to be condemned to long periods of privatization during which they live through an impoverishing 'atrophy of public meanings,' followed by spasmodic outbursts of 'publicness' that are hardly likely to be constructive."[19]

Political Economy and Supranationalism

G LOBAL forces buffeting the American economy reduce each person's sense of control over the present and the future. At the same time, supranationalism diminishes government's ability to influence the direction of change in the national economy. The individual feeling of loss of control leads to a retreat into personal survival—"meism"—that precludes a consideration of the common good. In public policy, loss of national control shows up in a re-emergence of political and economic nationalism as compensation for the decline in the government's legitimate responsibility in economic affairs.

While an unprecedented process of globalization is occurring in the world economy, the compensatory reaction to this supranationalism is a devolution into preoccupations with the self, at the expense of the community, combined with political chauvinism and economic protectionism in the nation-state, at the expense of international cooperation. "The ideological claims made for the private life," says Albert Hirschman of Princeton's Institute for Advanced Study, "sustain the individual's quest with two messages: one, the promise of satisfaction and happiness; and two, the assurance that there is no need for guilt feelings or regrets over the neglect of public life."[20]

Neither meism nor economic nationalism, however, is an answer to the supranational forces that disrupt economic life. Today, the world suffers from what Fred Hirsch says is the "tragedy of the commons. Everyone benefits from the upkeep of the common, but no one has the motivation to tend it himself, so there develops the opposite and fatal incentive to graze and overgraze it before others complete its ruin."[21] The problem is not an absence of public policy remedies that will restore some balance between private pursuits and the public good. Rather, it is the pendulum swing of politics toward an extreme form of what Hirsch calls "the tyranny of small decisions": an inability to exercise our imagination about how a world economy can function in the interests both of individuals and the commons.[22]

The danger is that by neglecting the public good, in an overly zealous pursuit of private self-aggrandizement, the world is simply marking time before a serious economic crisis occurs that cannot be contained by crisis management. Then Fred Hirsch's warning, issued in 1976, will have even more urgency:

It is now questionable whether the road to the carefree society can run through the market economy, dominated as it is by piecemeal choices exercised by individuals in response to their immediate situation. The choices offered by market opportunities are justly celebrated as liberating for the individual. Unfortunately, individual liberation does not make them liberating for all individuals together.[23]

PUBLIC POLICY FOR A
SUPRANATIONAL ORDER

A T A TIME when there is a need for more integration of public policy across national borders, private supranationalism is driving the world economy toward economic nationalism. Supranationalism contributes to the nation-state's loss of influence over its own economic affairs. It breeds national protectionist policies, as compensation for the absence of effective public policy strategies that can compete with private supranationalism. This shows up most clearly in global finance: "Today, the pace and pattern of world credit growth are determined by the hopes and judgments of international banks, investors, and corporate officials—not sitting as a single responsible body but acting in the involuntary unison that emerges from the competition of the marketplace," argues the economist Robert Heilbroner. "There is a good deal to be said for market outcomes in many areas, but not in that of international finance."[1]

As a result of supranationalism, Heilbroner continues, "the problems of international trade and finance
. . . bring to many the uneasy suspicion that the basic
unit of economic policy—the nation state—is not appropriate to the problems of late-twentieth-century capitalism."[2] Economic instability and worldwide economic
austerity are the consequences of what the Committee
on Energy and Commerce of the House of Representatives describes as "an integrated world financial/mone-
tary market system," but with "no world monetary or
financial authority capable of managing that system."[3]
Confronted by these seemingly impenetrable global
forces, the "entrenchment of the individualist ethos" occurs, says the social critic Fred Hirsch, at the same time
as "management of the system has become more necessary."[4] Wedded to outmoded mythologies, politics has
failed to address adequately the new global realities of
the 1980s. Like beached whales, both liberals and conservatives have been stranded by a tide that has
changed.

The central problem for American society, between
now and the end of this century, is to find a means of
integrating the pursuit of private pleasure, exercised
through the market, with a common concern for the
public good, articulated through the political system.
This dilemma has faced every generation since the Industrial Revolution, but it is given a unique urgency by
the new supranational institutions that threaten to ele-
vate permanently private pursuits over the public good.
Neither private pursuits nor the public good is advanced
by one extreme or the other, free-market obsessions or
rigid bureaucratic public management.

To resolve these competing political-economic objectives, the nations of the world must first acquire some
room for reflection and maneuver. William Keegan of the
Observer, in challenging what he calls the TINA position

("There is no alternative"), says: "I myself have always believed that if you are driving over the edge of a cliff, the priority is to question the direction in which you are travelling; the many different ways of driving away from the edge are a secondary consideration."[5]

Restoring Monetary Stability

THE HEADLINE "Ohio S & Ls Closed by Governor" that greeted readers of their morning newspapers in mid-March 1985 was followed in May by the Maryland banking crisis, almost a year to the day after news was broadcast about Continental Illinois's inability to meet the run on its deposits. Governor Richard F. Celeste's decision to close all seventy savings and loan banks in Ohio for a week was the first "bank holiday" in the United States since President Franklin D. Roosevelt took similar action in 1933, when he shut down all the banks in the United States, until time could defuse a speculative panic that threatened the entire financial system. Banks run on credit, and the Latin derivation for this word is *credere*, "to believe." It is becoming increasingly apparent, however, that the credibility of the banking system is being questioned by a skeptical public.

In what has become an annual spring ritual, as regular as the appearance of the first crocuses, the financial authorities and private banks mobilize to prevent a minor bank run from becoming the "mouse that roared," starting an avalanche of deposit withdrawals that cannot be contained. How many times has the public been reassured in the 1980s about the solvency of the financial system, after one of these bank crises, only to be blindsided by some new problem in a remote corner of the world's financial edifice? The financial house of cards may not come tumbling down, but the measures needed to prop it up are antithetical to a sound economy. Prudent reforms are needed to free public policy from the limited options imposed on the economy by deregulated, free-market monetarist austerity.

The excessive supply of unregulated Eurodollars and Third World debt are merely opposite sides of the same coin. They both arose, in large part, because of international monetary deregulation after Bretton Woods, which is also the source of exchange rate instability. The *Economist* points out, for example, that the wild swings in exchange rates are "influenced mainly by flows of money that have nothing to do with international trade. In 1984, world trade was worth about $2 trillion; financial flows were worth anywhere between $20 trillion and $50 trillion."[6] Quieting worldwide financial instability requires a strategy that simultaneously addresses both the Eurodollar overhang and Third World debt, in the context of a *re*-regulation of international money.

The $550 billion debt owed at the end of 1984 by less-developed countries, Eastern European nations, and the Soviet Union to private supranational banks cannot be repaid in its present form. The time horizon is too short for the debtor nations to accumulate the hard currency they need to pay off this amount of debt in the austere, monetarist economic environment that pervades the world economy. The consequence is a lunging from crisis to crisis that is destabilizing for both debtor and creditor nations. To extricate ourselves from this game of chicken being played with blindfolds requires an institutionalized process of orderly debt rescheduling.

Such a plan involves, first, the establishment of a new

public debt authority, which acts like a financial intermediary and is initially subscribed through public allocations that would otherwise go toward short-term private-bank bailouts. With this public endowment in hand, the new public debt authority can then leverage its capital in additional borrowing from the Eurodollar system. Whether it is some existing institution, like the IMF or World Bank, or a new financial authority is a technical question that is not terribly important. One appealing prospect is to place this authority under joint management by the World Bank and IMF, which have substantial knowledge of the problem but approach it from different perspectives. What is of consequence, however, is the broad policy guidelines for this new financial intermediary.

With funds borrowed from the Eurodollar market, the public debt authority would then reschedule international debt by offering to buy existing debt obligations from the supranational banks. Under some proposals, the public debt authority would buy the debts dollar-for-dollar with its own low-interest, long-term bonds; under other proposals, the debt would be bought for cash at less than its face value by central banks.[7] Both result in some loss of current income for the private banks, but as Felix Rohatyn, a New York investment banker, points out: "Because of greater safety of the credit, their regulators could permit them to schedule limited write-downs over a long period of time."[8] A reasonable scheme would give the private banks a choice: either accept cash at less than face value from their central bank or instead take long-term bonds issued by the public debt authority that carry lower rates of interest than are presently being earned on the existing risky debts.

The debtor countries would then have to deal with the public debt authority that now holds their debt. Rescheduling could take place in an orderly fashion, before a crisis stage is reached and on terms that more accurately reflect the real character of these debt obligations. When the debt is rescheduled, it could be stretched out over a longer time span than is now being done, enabling it to be paid off in smaller annual sums but for a longer period of time. Unlike a private supranational bank, the public debt authority would be under no obligation to show short-term quarterly profit increases to Wall Street.

A second stabilizing benefit of this proposal is the reduction of the Eurodollar overhang. As an initial step in placing some of the Eurodollars under public control, the scheme for a public-debt-rescheduling authority fulfills the objective of reducing the excessive supply of footloose supranational money that, left to its own devices, tends to destabilize the world economy.

Coupled with this by-product of the debt-rescheduling plan, private supranational banks should come under more regulatory authority as a quid pro quo for this one-time bailout. The first regulation is a reserve requirement against Eurodollar accounts. A reserve requirement on Eurodollars has two effects: first, it slows down the rate of growth of supranational money; and, second, it makes the Eurodollar system less profitable for supranational banks. In this way, a reserve requirement restores public influence over international money. It could be smaller than, the same as, or higher than reserve requirements on domestic accounts, depending on how sharply Eurodollar growth is to be curtailed. If higher than reserve requirements on domestic accounts, the rate of growth of supranational money can be quickly reduced and the rate of repatriation back to the United States accelerated.

Such a policy measure requires no new legislation or international agreements. It can be done by the Federal Reserve under its existing authority. All that is needed is the political will to resist the enormous political pressure from the banks. What the banks achieve, however, is extrication from a situation that threatens them with massive losses. Under an orderly debt-rescheduling scheme, the losses are minimized and made predictable. In return for this, the banks will have to accept reserve requirements on their Eurodollar accounts as a condition for the public bailout they recieve, just as they impose conditions on countries that reschedule their debts through them.

The private supranational banks must also provide more timely and accurate reporting about their international activities. Presently, they have to report less about their international operations than virtually any other business, large or small. The institutional development of a supranational banking system has far exceeded the information base of those U.S. government agencies that are charged with safeguarding the banking system. More reporting redresses this imbalance.

This comprehensive scheme for restoring international monetary stability treats simultaneously the multiple problems that presently plague the world financial system: an orderly rescheduling of international debt, a reduction of the Eurodollar overhang, and a re-regulation of international money. At the same time, it restores the legitimate bank monitoring functions of the public by requiring more reporting. By placing reserve requirements on supranational money and by bringing them under the umbrella of public control, the reforms are designed to eliminate the root cause of imprudent international loans and excessive expansion of international money. This policy strategy restores a legitimate public regulatory authority over money that even the most doctrinaire laissez-faire economist should accept as an appropriate government function. It does so in a responsible way, encouraging sacrifices by all parties, but without the destabilizing effect of either debt defaults or harsh rescheduling conditions imposed in the midst of a financial crisis.

Greater monetary stability has to be purchased at everyone's expense, but in a way that shares the burdens more equitably than in the present ad hoc crisis-management mode. Where this plan differs from others under discussion is in the restoration of public regulatory authority over supranational money. Without such institutional reforms, however, the other schemes for debt rescheduling merely buy a little time, without resolving the underlying cause of international financial instability: unregulated supranational money.

International Trade in Economic and Social Policy

I NTERNATIONAL trade is conventionally thought of in terms of the movement of goods and services across national borders. Alongside such trade, there is also a transfer of public policies across national borders that takes on increasing importance during the present supranational period. American firms have lost competitiveness, the argument goes, because labor costs are too high and government regulations are too stringent, compared with the country's trade competitors. Implicit in such comparisons is a public policy stance that advocates importing into the United States some form of these looser regulatory policies and tighter labor controls from other countries, whose political systems may not be democratic and where trade unions may be illegal. While attractive to a business firm, such public policy institutions are at odds with the political-economic foundations of the United States and are incompatible with American laws. Is the U.S. supposed to accept Philippine labor costs or Chilean pollution controls as the standard against which the country's public policies are judged?

The Committee on Energy and Commerce of the House of Representatives answered this question by saying the country should not join what they call a "race to the bottom" in which "nations are forced to compete for investment by undercutting one another" on economic and social policy. "To say that we should solve our trade problems by lowering our own wages is tantamount to saying that in order to compete with poor countries we must ourselves agree to be poor. Such a view is nonsensical and defeats the very purpose of economic policy—increasing wealth and prosperity."[9]

In return for imports of economic and social policies from countries with a more favorable business climate, the United States, in the supranational period, exports free-market, monetarist austerity. This is done through IMF conditionality, high-interest rate policies in the U.S. that have to be matched abroad by other industrial countries, and the advocacy of free-market policies in international institutions, like the World Bank and other regional banks.

It is impossible to draw up an accounting balance for this trade in economic and social policy. To the extent that a nation's sovereignty is breached by such trade, no country can claim an advantage. The movement of public policies across national boundaries is yet another way in which the supranational system breaks down national sovereignty and weakens public policy formation. When this occurs, free-market economics is strengthened and any attempt to reach an appropriate compromise between private pursuits and the public good becomes more difficult. In this environment, liberal political economy is forced to retreat in the face of a free-market juggernaut that appears to be unstoppable by public policy.

Part of the reason for this is the appeal of simplicity that free-market solutions offer. The subtlety and complexity involved with balancing the society appear to be too cumbersome during a swing of the political pendulum away from concerns about the common good. This leads to the classic "free rider" problem: "The rational individualist, in situations of social interdependence, knows that he does best when everyone *else* cooperates and he does not. . . ." [10] Everyone cannot be a free rider, however, or the social fabric disintegrates. "The pursuit of private and essentially individualistic economic goals," says Fred Hirsch, "must be girded at key points by a strict social morality," and the purpose of public policy is to "create the conditions in which individualistic calculation can continue to operate in a socially benign way." [11]

International trade in economic and social policy feeds a process of individualism that tends to weaken the public good. It is justified by free-trade ideology, which is an extension of free-market economics into international economics. Differences in product cost, however, that are due to totalitarian political institutions or restrictions on economic rights reflect no natural or entrepreneurial advantage. The textbook doctrine of free trade is based either on natural endowments or productivity advantages that accrue from more-advanced technology or superior management. It implicitly assumes comparable institutions among trading nations. Free trade has nothing to do with incomparable political-economic institutions that protect individual rights in one country and deny them in another. Such distortions of free-trade doctrine can be legitimately corrected by U.S. trade policy, thereby strengthening the force of human rights appeals.

"While realism requires flexibility in the face of international competition," says the House Energy and Commerce Committee, "the U.S. cannot agree to abandon its standard of living" in the name of a free-trade ideology, when it derives from the absence of freedom in our trading competitors.[12] A compensatory surcharge on imports from totalitarian countries strengthens the world political economy, without degenerating into arbitrary protectionism. Moreover, it does not breach the boundaries of a trade policy that encourages the freest movement of goods and services, consistent with the principles of equitable competition in international trade.

Mobilizing Capital for Productive Investment

T HE SUPRANATIONAL economic system breeds unproductive investment in short-term paper assets, at the expense of investment in tangible capital assets that leads to economic growth and higher employment. The measures that bring supranational money under the umbrella of public policy, and impose a cost on totalitarianism in international trade, go far toward arresting this tendency. An additional policy strategy is needed, however, to address the problem of mergers and acquisitions that divert financial resources from productive capital investment projects.

Mergers and acquisitions, which immobilized nearly $450 billion between 1979 and 1984, are the most transparent form of short-term speculation in paper assets during the supranational era. Some mergers and acquisitions have a longer-term productive purpose, and they should be encouraged. What should be discouraged, however, are the Gamesmen-driven mergers and acquisitions that reflect purely short-term speculation and personal self-aggrandizement.

Capital gains that accrue from the sale of a stock of a company involved in a merger or acquisition during a period six months before and six months after the consummation of a merger or acquisition should be taxed at the normal higher income tax rate and not at the lower capital gains rate. The normal income tax rate would be applied at the time of sale of the stock and does not depend on when the stock was initially purchased. This places short-term gain from financial speculation on a par with normal income and removes the special lower capital gains tax on these forms of stock manipulation. However, if higher profits are earned from genuine new productive potential and occur beyond the six months after a merger or acquisition, the usual lower capital gains tax prevails. Mergers and acquisitions that have a long-term productive potential, therefore, are still encouraged by this tax change. In fact, they now become more important in the merger and acquisition business because of the preferred tax treatment on the higher profits after the six-month waiting period. Speculative gains from mergers and acquisitions, however, based solely on an inflation of stock values for only a very short period of time, are discouraged by this policy.

This tax change restores the true public policy purpose of the capital gains tax: tax relief justified by the gain for society as a whole, through the capital formation that leads to economic growth and employment. However, this rationale for a lower tax on capital gains should not be applied to the type of financial gamesmanship involved with many mergers and acquisitions. In these situations, the incentive to make huge profits on increases in stock values, a few months before and after a merger or acquisition, is reduced by taxing those gains at a higher rate than applies to capital gains that accrue over a longer period of time. In this way, financial capital that is now tied up in mergers and acquisitions should be freed to perform the functions expected of it in an industrial economy.

Transnational Economic Policy Coordination

T HE SUPRANATIONAL system has produced a closer integration of the private sectors of the world economy, but at the expense of national public policy, which has disintegrated as supranationalism has expanded. After the end of Bretton Woods, say Robert D. Putnam and Nicholas Bayne, two international relations experts who have written about policy coordination among industrial countries, "the links between the industrial countries no longer suggested the image of climbers moving upwards securely roped together, but rather of prisoners shackled to one another deprived of their freedom of action."[13] A transnational policy strategy is needed, therefore, to deal with the new problems created by an integrated private world economy that, according to the Congressional Committee on Energy and Commerce, "has now far outstripped the development of international political mechanisms capable of exercising economic management."[14]

The reforms that bring supranational money under public policy influence, restructure international debt, discourage the unproductive use of capital in mergers and acquisitions, and balance international trade more equitably among countries reinforce the perspective of Helmut Schmidt, former chancellor of West Germany, and his finance minister, Manfred Lahnstein, who say: "The world economy . . . can only be steered by a joint effort" because "the 'self-healing powers of the market' cannot take care of all our problems." [15]

Two interconnected problems require a joint steering effort by the industrial democracies: exchange rate instability and excessively high interest rates. Neither can be solved by national policy alone, although each country thinks it can gain an advantage in the world economy, through its national economic policy, at the expense of every other country. In game theory, this is called the "prisoner's dilemma": "Every participant would be better off if collective action were taken, but . . . each, individually, has a powerful incentive to defect from the collective action and become a 'free rider.' " [16] However, as exchange rate instability and high interest rates destabilize more economies and make the world financial system more precarious, there is a developing consensus around the need for collaborative transnational policy responses to the problems thrown forth by supranationalism. The September 22, 1985 initiative among the so-called G-5 countries (United States, West Germany, Japan, France, and Great Britain) to intervene in foreign exchange markets reversed the previous laissez-faire policy and was a tentative step toward transnational policy coordination. No country is able to avoid the destabilizing forces produced by unregulated supranationalism: "If the world economy is in disarray," say Schmidt and Lahnstein, "no country can be, or remain, an island of stability. It is a mistake to believe that any government can pursue whatever economic policy seems domestically expedient without regard for other countries."[17]

To provide more exchange rate stability and predictability, target zones should be established. Such bands would permit more room for exchange rate fluctuation and adjustment than existed under Bretton Woods but less volatility than presently exists under freely floating exchange rates. Since there are only four currency blocs that matter in the world financial system—the U.S. dollar, the Japanese yen, British sterling, and the European Monetary System (which is primarily organized around the German mark)—agreement is needed only among this relatively small group of countries.

In the European Monetary System, an exchange rate stabilization scheme is already in place and works quite effectively. The Japanese are very pliant about international financial issues and can be expected to go along with whatever the Americans propose so long as its trade balance is not seriously affected. Only the United States and Great Britain resist schemes for exchange rate stabilization, but the British are rather isolated in their incompatible position as a member of the European Economic Community and a holdout from the European Monetary System.

It is not surprising, therefore, that the American dollar and the British pound have suffered the greatest instability since the establishment of the European Monetary System. The tens of billions of roaming supranational monies need a short-term speculative target. However imprecise is the economic management of Thatcher and Reagan, nothing they have done justifies a 25 percent fall in the pound against the dollar in the last six months of 1984, followed by a 33 percent rise in the pound during the next six months. Supranational money requires substantial play in the foreign exchange markets for speculation to be profitable. Inevitably, one country's currency will come under attack, followed by some other country's currency when the markets pursue another target.

Conveniently, representatives from the industrial countries have several existing venues for ongoing meetings about mutual economic problems at the Organization for Economic Cooperation and Development, IMF committees, and the annual economic summits among the heads of state. With an institutional infrastructure already in place for discussions about exchange rate problems, the leaders of the industrial countries lack only the political commitment to do something about excessive exchange rate volatility.

The technical argument against the feasibility of target zone exchange rates is based on the difficulties caused by the enormous sums in Eurodollar accounts that could overwhelm the resources of the stabilization policy. If the proposals presented earlier in this chapter to reduce the Eurodollar overhang are implemented, however, this objection to the scheme is answered. At present, the vast sums of footloose Eurodollars comprise what is called "hot money"—currencies that move instantaneously around the world and create speculative cycles in exchange rates that do not reflect underlying economic realities. Intervention by a stabilization strategy would be nullified by the tens of billions of supranational dollars, unless the stabilization fund had comparable resources to throw at exchange rate speculation. But no proposal for target zones contemplates a stabilization war chest that could compete with private supranational money. As these sums are reduced by reserve requirements, however, the amount of speculative Eurodollars will be diminished, thereby permitting an exchange rate stabilization mechanism to work. In fact, without such prior policy measures, it is hard to see

how any stabilization fund could challenge the speculators and their quantities of supranational money. The
key, therefore, to a new exchange rate stabilization system is restoring public regulatory influence over the private supranational monetary system.

Exchange rate instability is a major cause of high interest rates. They are the only effective weapon against
short-term exchange rate fluctuations, and countries
play the interest rate card whenever their currencies
come under attack. The result is a competitive worldwide ratcheting up of interest rates that reduces economic growth, makes debt repayment out of reach for
many debtor nations, and is generally dysfunctional for
nearly everyone. The measures that produce more-stable
exchange rates, therefore, will reduce the tendency toward high interest rates that has dominated economies
in the 1980s. No longer will the interest rate have to go
up in one country in response to a weakening of its
currency, raising the ante for the next country whose
currency comes under attack, and so on, until the average rate of interest is higher than can be justified by
current inflation or expectations about the future. However, this is precisely the way in which the monetary
policy game has been played in the 1980s.

Supranational money moves around the world on a
short-term basis, seeking the highest rate of return,
tempered by risk. The comparative rate of interest paid
in one country versus another is, therefore, the major
indicator used by speculators to decide where to put
their cash on any given day and during any particular
hour of day. It is not the average rate of interest among
all the countries in the world that speculators look at,
but the relative rates. They cause the movements of
money in and out of currencies that then show up in
the nightly exchange rate figures reported on newscasts.
Even with more-stable exchange rates, a way has to be

found to move from the present structure of relative interest rates, built around a high level of interest rates, to a structure built around a lower average interest rate that is more compatible with economic fundamentals.

In the 1980s, a speculative bulge appeared in average interest rates that was caused by the need for each nation, acting separately, to defend its currency by raising interest rates. National monetary policy was distorted by the absence of a transnational approach to exchange rate fluctuation. The transnational policy objective is to maintain relative rates of interest, while reducing the average level of interest in the world economy so that it more closely reflects inflation and future expectations. No country can do this alone; in fact, all an individual country can do is make matters worse by placing an ever-higher floor under interest rates. It is the classic prisoner's dilemma problem, and only a transnational resolution is possible.

An agreement to remove the speculative bulge in interest rates is like the twice-yearly resetting of our clocks. Everyone agrees to change them at a specified time, on a specified day, and in a moment time has been reset in the world. Resetting the interest rate would be easy if the nations of the world could treat it like the resetting of clocks. Although the process is not quite this simple, there is no reason why a competitive upward ratcheting of interest rates among the industrial nations cannot be reversed by a symmetric downward ratcheting of interest rates through transnational policy coordination.

Gradually, the average rate of interest should be lowered by the industrial nations, consistent with the economic fundamentals of inflation and expectations. They should agree to maintain specified relative interest rates, during this downward adjustment period, so long as exchange rates can be maintained within the target zones. A deviation from a target zone, that cannot be corrected through other interventions, would indicate that a country's interest rate is out of line. Under these circumstances, an interest rate adjustment can occur within a transnational consultative structure.

If this scenario was for a movie, one scene would fade out and another would fade in. Ideally, the directors of transnational policy would like to have the powers of a film director. They do not, and management of a reset interest rate structure requires a subtle touch. It is more like re-tuning an engine that has been performing poorly. One adjustment is made, and the mechanic waits to see what happens before making the next adjustment, continuing until it works properly.

Such policy management is within the reach of governments. Achieving more stable exchange rates and a lower average level of interest rates, through transnational policy coordination, compares favorably with the more difficult crisis management of today, where policy administrators have to improvise new tactics in the midst of possible financial panic. To those who say it cannot be done, the question has to be asked: why not? And if not, what is the alternative? Putnam and Bayne, who have made a study of the economic summits among heads of state, provide this answer:

Interdependence has created an ever sharper dilemma for democratically elected politicians. The fate of a congressman from Youngstown depends on decisions taken in Brussels or Tokyo. The *projet* of a French socialist president is constrained by decisions of U.S. monetary authorities. . . . In such predicaments governments must choose some mix of two broad strategies, one nationalist, one internationalist. They may try to regain control over their own destiny, by re-erecting protectionist barriers to international commerce and finance. . . . Or they may seek instead to cooperate with their counterparts abroad in an effort to manage politically the mutual interference that is the price of interdependence.[18]

A Reconstruction of Political Economy

T HE REFORMS proposed in this chapter bring the supranational economy under a degree of public control, without disturbing the useful functions performed by this system. Only the excesses, which destabilize national economies and the world economy, are regulated. Supranational money and its growth are regulated through reserve requirements on Eurodollar accounts that bring them into line with domestic accounts. This is a regulation that is widely accepted and has been used for decades on domestic accounts, not only in the U.S., but in other countries as well. Banks are required to report more about their activities so regulators will be able to take preventive measures and avoid another Ohio or Continental Illinois. International debt is rescheduled in an orderly way without relaxing vigilance over the management of the economies of debtor nations. The Eurodollar overhang is reduced both by the reserve requirement and the borrowing by the debt-rescheduling authority.

Greater exchange rate stability is achieved by controlling the major source of short-term instability: the growth of unregulated Eurodollars. A new target zone exchange rate system is also proposed that will provide the predictability in international economic relations that is now absent. After exchange rates are stabilized, a reduction in the average level of interest rates becomes feasible, compatible with inflation and expectations. Relative rates of interest among different countries are retained, consistent with the maintenance of the target zone exchange rates, while the average rate of interest is gradually lowered.

A lower average rate of interest should encourage more long-term productive investment, and the reduction in speculative short-term financial resources in the world economy should also contribute to the mobilization of investment in tangible assets. A balance of political-economic policies is introduced into trading relations in the international economy by reducing the financial benefits that accrue from totalitarianism. As a final measure, designed to mobilize resources for productive investment and discourage short-term financial gamesmanship, the capital gains tax is altered. Mergers and acquisitions that simply rearrange existing assets are penalized, while those that have a longer-term productive payoff for the economy are encouraged.

Some of these changes can be accomplished by the United States, acting alone. Others require transnational collaborative arrangements that can readily be implemented through existing structures. This strategy constrasts with a call for a second Bretton Woods by some political leaders, academics, and policy makers.[19] While appealing at first glance, the problem with a second Bretton Woods is the complications created by a general meeting of this sort. Issues of representation, agenda, voting, and so on could paralyze such a gathering and add fuel to the there-is-no-alternative position of the opponents of international economic reform. The problems are too serious to invite any distractions from the main issue of how the world political economy can be restructured to support economic growth and employment. The proposals for reform in this chapter are simple, have been tested in one form or another, and require a minimun of bureaucratic intervention. In short, they are eminently feasible and are compatible with the world's existing administrative and policy structures.

The new balance of economic policies in the world economy would open up the possibility of replacing monetarist austerity with economic growth and employment. In this new environment of regulated supranationalism, the concrete problems of employment and growth return to center stage, and the abstract-symbol economy of money and credit recedes into the background. The debate over political economy, between liberals and conservatives, can also be conducted in a different context once these changes are realized.

Presently, on the one side, a new conservatism offers more of the same: crisis management, deregulation, and free-market solutions. On the other, an old liberalism, rooted in the experience of the 1930s and 1960s, offers protection to those cast aside by the supranational economic order but has no resolution of the central problem of supranationalism. Neither one can contend effectively with the powerful juggernaut of technological change and modernization that is uprooting lives and changing the way in which the economy works. Conservatives simply permit these developments to unfold, no matter what their consequences. Liberals take a defensive posture that appears to align them against change and in support of a new Luddism.

The task for a reconstructed liberalism is to ride the crest of the wave of modernization, while providing the public policy context that permits people to adjust without subjecting them solely to the mercy of market forces. Such modernization with a human face is within reach, but only after unregulated supranationalism is encompassed by public policy. A political economy can then be contemplated that restores equilibrium between the private pursuit of personal gain in the market and the promotion of the common good through government.

The twentieth century is entering its last decade in a form that is unrecognizable from the first decade of the century. Change has become the norm, not the exception. From a time when major technological transformations occurred every quarter century, they now happen each decade. The rapidity of the turnover of technologies has left institutions behind, incapable of handling new problems with arrangements suited to earlier, outmoded technologies.

In the world economy, a private supranationalism, energized by the technological revolution in information and communications, has overwhelmed public institutions that were designed for what now looks like a horse-and-buggy technological era. Filling this gap, between private technological modernism and public institutional obsolescence, is free-market monetarism—a political-economic strategy that, at best, holds the system together for a short time but is unable to produce the structural changes that are needed to place it on a more solid footing. The alternative to this nineteenth-century, free-market utopia is public institutional innovation, which rivals the ingenuity of private supranationalism and prepares the world economy for entry into the twenty-first century.

NOTES

Preface

1. "Stateless Money. A New Force on World Economies," *Business Week* (August 21, 1978), pp. 76, 77, 80.

2. Susan Strange, *International Economic Relations of the Western World, 1958–1971. International Monetary Relations* (Oxford: Oxford University Press, 1976), p. 25.

3. Ibid.

Chapter 1. Ways of Thinking About the Supranational Economy

1. U.S. Federal Reserve, *Federal Reserve Bulletin* (January 1981), p. A24; and Council of Economic Advisers, *Economic Report of the President, 1984* (Washington: Government Printing Office, 1984), p. 255

2. Statement by Senator Hubert H. Humphrey on the International Development Cooperation Act of 1978, *Congressional Record*, 95th Congress, 124, 5 (January 25, 1978).

3. " 'Made in U.S.A.' Means Little to the Multinationals," *Business Week* (April 10, 1978), p. 60.

4. Ralph Kozlow, "Capital Expenditures by Majority-Owned Foreign Affiliates of U.S. Companies, 1985," *Survey of Current Business*, 65, 3 (March 1985), p. 24; and Council of Economic Advisers, *Economic Report of the President, 1985* (Washington: Government Printing Office, 1985), p. 232.

5. Susan J. Tolchin and Martin Tolchin, *Dismantling America. The Rush to Deregulate* (Boston: Houghton Mifflin Co., 1983), p. 3.

6. Richard J. Barnet and Ronald E. Muller, *Global Reach. The Power of the Multinational Corporation* (New York: Simon & Schuster, 1974), pp. 13, 15–16.

7. Lester C. Thurow, *The Zero Sum Society* (New York: Basic Books, 1980); Fred Hirsch, *The Social Limits to Growth* (Cambridge: Harvard University Press, 1976); Andrew Shonfield, *The Use of Public Power* (Oxford: Oxford University Press, 1982); and Mancur Olson, *The Rise and Decline of Nations* (New Haven: Yale University Press, 1982).

8. David P. Calleo, *The Imperious Economy* (Cambridge: Harvard University Press, 1982); C. Fred Bergsten, "The United States and the World Economy," *Annals of the American Academy of Political and Social Science*, 460 (March 1982), pp. 11–20; and Ira C. Magaziner and Robert B. Reich, *Minding America's Business* (New York: Random House, 1982).

9. J. W. Anderson, "More and More, It's a Global Game," *Washington Post* (January 2, 1983), p. B8.

10. Bergsten, "The United States and the World Economy," p. 12.

11. World Bank, *World Development Report 1985* (Oxford: Oxford University Press, 1985), p. 23.

12. Seymour Zucker, "An OPEC Price Crash Can't Be Bad News," *Business Week* (February 7, 1983), p 36.

13. Bergsten, "The United States and the World Economy," p. 13.

14. Michael Dobbs, "Dreams Fade to Reality for French Socialists," *Washington Post* (November 22, 1983), p. A1.

15. Morton M. Kondracke, "Restoring Control: Ronald Reagan's Electoral Mandate," *Wall Street Journal* (December 18, 1980), p. 28.

16. Robert J. Samuelson, "Across the Nation a Feeling of Unease," *Washington Post* (March 28, 1984), p. D7-8.

17. Robert Heilbroner, "Economic Prospects," *New Yorker* (August 29, 1983), p. 78.

18. Paul P. Streeten, "What New International Economic Order?," *Ordnungspolitische Fragen Zum Nord-Sud Konflikt* (Berlin: Duncker & Humblot, 1983), p. 83.

19. Celso Furtado, "Crisis and Change in the World Economy," Committee for Development Planning (May, 1984), p. 3.

20. David Edwards, "The Trading Room," *MBA Magazine* (June/July 1978), p. 13.

21. "Survey of International Banking," *Economist* (March 24, 1984), p. 10.

22. Peter F. Drucker, "Schumpeter and Keynes," *Forbes* (May 23, 1983), p. 125.

23. Paul P. Streeten, "Proposal for the Establishment of an International Economic Policy Research Institute," United Nations University (August 4, 1981), p. 2.

24. J. W. Anderson, "Why the Numbers Lied," *Washington Post Book World* (May 22, 1983), p. 9.

25. Streeten "What New International Economic Order?," p. 82.

Chapter 2. Bretton Woods, 1944

1. Hobart Rowen, "Bretton Woods Revisited," *Washington Post* (July 15, 1984), p. G1.

2. Morgenthau was a meticulous diarist, and his diaries provide an extraordinary glimpse into decision making in the Roosevelt administration. This quotation and others in this chapter from Morgenthau's diaries appear in: Armand Van Dormael, *Bretton Woods. Birth of a Monetary System* (New York: Holmes & Meier, 1978), p. 40.

3. Roy F. Harrod, *The Life of John Maynard Keynes* (London: Macmillan & Co., 1951), pp. 557–58.

4. *New Yorker* (May 21, 1984), p. 64.

5. Van Dormael, *Bretton Woods*, p. 154.

6. Rowen, "Bretton Woods Revisited," p. G4.

7. Paul P. Streeten, "What New International Economic Order?," *Ordnungspolitische Fragen Zum Nord-Sud-Konflikt* (Berlin: Duncker & Humblot, 1984), p. 82.

8. Aphra Behn, *The Rover*, pt. III, act 1.

9. "International Finance and Power," *Monthly Review*, 35, 5 (October 1983), p. 8.

10. Susan Strange, *Sterling and British Policy. A Political Study of an International Currency in Decline* (Oxford: Oxford University Press, 1971), p. 6.

11. David P. Calleo and Benjamin M. Rowland, *America and the World Economy. Atlantic Dreams and National Realities* (Bloomington: Indiana University Press, 1973), p. 6.

12. Van Dormael, *Bretton Woods*, p. 1.

13. Ibid., pp. 94–95, 208, 209.

14. David P. Calleo, *The Imperious Economy* (Cambridge: Harvard University Press, 1982), p. 1.

15. Charles P. Kindelberger, *Manias, Panics, and Crashes. A History of Financial Crises* (New York: Basic Books, 1978), pp. 161–62.

16. Calleo and Rowland, *America and the World Economy*, p. 87; and Strange, *Sterling and British Policy*, p. 1.

Chapter 3. The Politics of International Money

1. John Maynard Keynes, "The Treaty of Peace," reprinted in his *Essays in Persuasion* (New York: W. W. Norton and Co., 1963), pp. 28, 36.

2. *Finance and Development* (March, 1984), p. 26; and Edward S. Mason and Robert E. Asher, *The World Bank Since Bretton Woods* (Washington, D.C.: The Brookings Institution, 1973), p. 5.

3. Armand Van Dormael, *Bretton Woods. Birth of a Monetary System* (New York: Holmes & Meier, 1978), pp. 261, 263.

4. Ibid., pp. 248, 249.

5. Ibid., p. 246.

6. David Rees, *Harry Dexter White. A Study in Paradox* (New York: Coward, McCann, & Geoghegan, 1973), chap. 15.

7. U.S. Department of Commerce, *International Direct Investment. Global Trends and the U.S. Role* (Washington: Government Printing Office, 1984), p. 6.

8. Van Dormael, *Bretton Woods*, p. 211.

9. Ibid., p. 132.

10. Council of Economic Advisers, *Economic Report of the President, 1984* (Washington: Government Printing Office, 1984), p. 332.

11. David P. Calleo and Benjamin M. Rowland, *America and the World Economy. Atlantic Dreams and National Realities* (Bloomington: Indiana University Press, 1973), p. 91.

12. David P. Calleo, *The Imperious Economy* (Cambridge: Harvard University Press, 1982), p. 47.

13. Calleo and Rowland, *America and the World Economy*, p. 87.

14. Calleo, *The Imperious Economy*, p. 83.

15. Van Dormael, *Bretton Woods*, p. 200.

16. On this, see the excellent biography of White: David Rees, *Harry Dexter White*.

17. Van Dormael, *Bretton Woods*, p. 219.

Chapter 4. Pax Americana Economica Unravels

1. David P. Calleo, *The Imperious Economy* (Cambridge: Harvard University Press, 1982), p. 166.

2. Ibid., p.3.

3. "The Road from Bretton Woods," *Economist* (September 27, 1980), p. 112.

4. Calleo, *The Imperious Economy*, p. 21.

5. U.S. Department of Commerce, *The Multinational Corporation* (Washington: Government Printing Office, 1972), p. 11.

6. Arthur M. Schlesinger, Jr., *A Thousand Days. John F. Kennedy in the White House* (Boston: Houghton Mifflin, 1965), pp. 652, 654.

7. Theodore C. Sorensen, *Kennedy* (New York: Harper & Row Publishers, 1965), p. 405.

8. Susan Strange, *International Economic Relations of the Western World, 1959–1971* (Oxford: Oxford University Press, 1976), p. 41.

9. Schlesinger, *A Thousand Days*, p. 654.

10. Sorensen, *Kennedy*, p. 408.

11. Strange, *International Economic Relations*, p. 286.

12. Ibid., pp. 283–85.

13. Ibid., p. 296.

14. Ibid., p. 288.

15. Lyndon Baines Johnson, *The Vantage Point. Perspectives on the Presidency 1963–1969* (New York: Holt, Rinehart & Winston, 1972), pp. 317, 319.

16. Strange, *International Economic Relations*, p. 335.

17. Joanne Gowa, *Closing the Gold Window. Domestic*

Politics and the End of Bretton Woods (Ithaca: Cornell University Press, 1983), p. 42.

18. Henry Kissinger, *The White House Years* (Boston: Little Brown, 1979), p. 951.

19. Gowa, *Closing the Gold Window*, p. 100.

20. Chuck Conconi, "Personalities," *Washington Post* (February 7, 1984), p. C3.

21. Gowa, *Closing the Gold Window*, p. 69.

22. Calleo, *The Imperious Economy*, p. 3.

23. Gowa, *Closing the Gold Window*, p. 137.

24. Kissinger, *The White House Years*, p. 955.

25. Strange, *International Economic Relations*, p. 339.

26. Susan Strange, "The Dollar Crisis 1971," *International Affairs*, 48, 2 (April 1972), p. 205.

27. Strange, *International Economic Relations*, p. 344.

28. "The Road From Bretton Woods," p. 115.

29. Strange, *International Economic Relations*, p. 344.

30. Ibid., p. 91.

Chapter 5. Supranational Money

1. Richard F. Janssen, "Rapid Growth of Eurodollar Market Prompts Debate over Wisdom of Imposing Controls," *Wall Street Journal* (August 3, 1979), p. 34.

2. Fritz Machlup, "Euro-Dollar Creation: A Mystery Story," *Banca Nazionale Del Lavoro Quarterly Review*, 94 (September 1970), p. 236.

3. Quoted in: Anthony Sampson, *The Money Lenders. The People and Politics of the World Banking Crisis* (London: Penguin Books, 1981), p.251.

4. Rainer S. Masera, "Recent Developments in the Economic Analysis of Euro-Markets," Bank for International Settlements, Monetary and Economic Department (September 1982), p. 3; and International Monetary Fund, *Annual Report 1983* (Washington: International Monetary Fund, 1983), p. 19.

5. "Stateless Money. A New Force on World Economies," *Business Week* (August 21, 1978), pp. 76, 77.

6. U.S. Congress, Joint Economic Committee, *Some Ques-*

tions and Brief Answers About the Eurodollar Market (Washington: Government Printing Office, 1977), p. 1.

7. James Gipson, "It's Only a Paper Economy . . . But It Defies the Bankers' Scissors," *Washington Post* (November 2, 1980), p. G20.

8. U.S. Congress, Committee On Banking, Currency, and Housing, *Financial Institutions and the Nation's Economy*, bk. II, pt. 4 (Washington: Government Printing Office, 1976), pp. 880, 883. Referred to hereafter as FINE.

9. Ibid., p. 898.

10. Janssen, "Rapid Growth of Eurodollar Market," p. 34.

11. Sampson, *The Money Lenders*, p. 137.

12. Janssen, "Rapid Growth of Eurodollar Market," p. 34.

13. Susan Strange, *Sterling and British Policy. A Political Study of an International Currency in Decline* (Oxford: Oxford University Press, 1971), pp. 203, 207.

14. Janssen, "Rapid Growth of Eurodollar Market," p. 34.

15. "Stateless Money," p. 76.

16. Paul Einzig, *Foreign Dollar Loans in Europe* (New York: St. Martin's Press, 1965), pp. vi, vii.

17. "Stateless Money," p. 78.

18. Joint Economic Committee, *Some Questions*, p. 2.

19. FINE, pp. 893, 894.

20. Gunter Dufey and Ian H. Giddy, *The International Money Market* (Englewood Cliffs: Prentice-Hall, 1978), p. 22.

21. "Stateless Money," p. 79.

22. Janssen, "Rapid Growth of Eurodollar Market," p. 34.

23. Ibid.

24. Robert Z. Aliber, *The International Money Game*, 4th ed. (New York: Basic Books, 1979), p. 167.

25. FINE, p. 816.

26. Dufey and Giddy, *The International Money Market*, p. 162.

27. Strange, *Sterling and British Policy*, p. 209.

28. International Monetary Fund, *Annual Report 1983*, p. 18.

29. FINE, p. 899.

30. S. C. Gwynne, "Adventures in the Loan Trade," *Harper's* (September 1983), p. 23.

31. Jackson Diehl, "Cautious Colombia Escapes Debt Crisis," *Washington Post* (May 22, 1984), p. A1.

32. Gwynne, "Adventures in the Loan Trade," p. 24.

33. Carlos Fuentes, "Rich Nations and Poor, Linked in Need," *Washington Post* (October 18, 1981), p. C5.

34. International Monetary Fund, *Annual Report 1983*, p. 18.

35. "The Realities of Interdependence," *Finance and Development* (March 1984), p. 31.

36. FINE, p. 806.

37. Ibid., p. 828.

38. R. M. Pecchioli, *The Internationalization of Banking. The Policy Issues* (Paris: OECD, 1983), p. 60.

39. Ann Crittenden, "Growing Bahamian Loan Activity by U.S. Banks Causes Concern," *New York Times* (March 3, 1977), p. 53.

40. "Banking Business Booms in the Bahamas," *New York Times* (March 3, 1977), p. 47.

41. Larry Kramer, "Public Gets First Glimpse of How U.S. Banks Utilize Their Offshore Tax Havens," *Washington Post* (December 24, 1978), p. H1.

42. "Banking Business Booms," p. 47; and Ann Crittenden, "Citibank Found to Lead in Shift to Tax Havens," *New York Times* (March 4, 1977), p. D5.

43. Bank for International Settlements, *Fifty-fifth Annual Report* (Basel: Bank for International Settlements, 1985), p. 115.

44. FINE, pp. 809, 811, 812.

45. Aliber, *The International Money Game*, p. 246.

46. Salomon Brothers, *United States Multinational Banking. Current and Prospective Strategies* (New York: Salomon Brothers, 1976), p. 3.

47. FINE, p. 892.

48. Crittenden, "Citibank Found to Lead," p. A1.

49. "Citibank's Pervasive Influence on International Lending," *Business Week* (May 16, 1983), p. 124.

50. Robert Heilbroner, "Economic Prospects," *New Yorker* (August 29, 1983), p. 70.

51. "The Glory Days Are Over at Citicorp," *Business Week*

(November 7, 1977), p. 65; and "Citibank's Pervasive Influence," p. 125.

52. Tom Herman, "Citibank Fact-Finding Study Indicates Possible Exposure to Foreign Tax Claims," *Wall Street Journal* (November 27, 1978), p. 4.

53. Kramer, "Public Gets First Glimpse," p. H5.

54. David Edwards, "The Trading Room," *MBA Magazine* (June/July 1978), p. 13.

55. Quoted in Larry Kramer, "International Money Trading Rapidly Growing Business," *Washington Post* (September 24, 1978), p. M3.

56. Ibid.

57. Deborah Rankin, "Fed Member Cool on Bank Plan for City," *New York Times* (May 23, 1978), p. D1.

58. E. J. Donne, Jr., "Tax Breaks on Overseas Loans Pushed for New York City Banks," *New York Times* (February 13, 1978), p. D6; and Crittenden, "Citibank Found to Lead," p. D5.

59. Pecchioli, *The Internationalization of Banking*, p. 63.

60. Morgan Guaranty Trust Company, *World Financial Markets* (January 1984), p. 5; and Federal Reserve Board, "Federal Reserve Statistical Release" (July 12, 1984), p. 3.

61. "Stateless Money," p. 76.

Chapter 6. Global Austerity

1. Calculated from: Council of Economic Advisers, *Economic Report of the President 1985* (Washington: Government Printing Office, 1985), pp. 291, 354.

2. World Bank, *Debt and the Developing World. Current Trends and Prospects* (Washington: World Bank, 1984), p. ix; and World Bank, *World Development Report 1985* (Oxford: Oxford University Press, 1985), p. 23.

3. John Newhouse, "The Diplomatic Round. One Against Nine," *New Yorker* (October 22, 1984), p. 64.

4. "Turn and Turn Again," *Observer* (December 9, 1984), p. 8.

5. Bank for International Settlements, *Fifty-fourth Annual*

Report (Basel: Bank for International Settlements, 1984), p. 80.

6. William Keegan, "Doing the Best to Abolish Business," *Observer* (December 30, 1984), p. 24.

7. "Recyclers' Recession," *Economist* (August 7, 1982), p. 12.

8. James Gipson, "Imprudent Bankers Count on Federal Aid," *Washington Post* (January 2, 1983), p. F7.

9. Hobart Rowen, "Loose Lending and the World Debt Crisis," *Washington Post* (September 19, 1982), p F1.

10. "Citibank's Pervasive Influence on International Lending," *Business Week* (May 16, 1983), p. 126.

11. Hobart Rowen, "Nine Major Banks Highly Exposed on Third World Loans," *Washington Post* (October 24, 1982), p. F1.

12. Norman A. Bailey, "An Insider's View: The Response of the Government of the United States to the International Debt Crisis 1981–83," Bildner Center for Western Hemisphere Studies, City University of New York (July 1984), pp. 2–3.

13. "Worry at the World's Banks," *Business Week* (September 6, 1982), p 83.

14. "William H. Rhodes on the Debt Crisis," *Washington Post* (August 19, 1984), p. G2.

15. "Why the Banks Bailed Out Peru," *Business Week* (March 21, 1977), p. 117.

16. Quoted in: U.S. House of Representatives, Committee on Banking, Currency, and Housing, *Financial Institutions and the Nation's Economy*, bk. II, pt. 4 (Washington: Government Printing Office, 1976), p. 901.

17. Arthur F. Burns, "The Need for Order in International Finance," Speech at the Annual Dinner of the Columbia University Graduate School of Business (April 12, 1977).

18. "William H. Rhodes on the Debt Crisis," p. G2.

19. Bailey, "An Insider's View," p. 5.

20. Jacques de Larosière, "Does the Fund Impose Austerity?," International Monetary Fund (June 1984), no page number.

21. "Recyclers' Recession," p. 13.

22. International Monetary Fund, *Annual Report 1980*, p. 110; and *Annual Report 1983*, p. 118 (Washington: International Monetary Fund, 1980, 1983).

23. World Bank, *Debt and the Developing World*, p. xviii; and World Bank, *World Development Report 1985*, p. 28.

24. Statement by Senator Bill Bradley of New Jersey to the European Management Forum, Davos, Switzerland (January 28, 1983), p. 1.

25. "Worry at the World's Banks," p. 82.

26. Leonard Rapping, "In the Financial Fast Lane," *New Leader* (October 17, 1983), p. 15.

27. Margot Hornblower, "Price Riots Imperil Dominican Government," *Washington Post* (April 30, 1984), p. A15.

28. "Worry at the World's Banks," p. 82.

29. Lawrence Rout, "Mexico Is Weathering the Float of the Peso, But Problems Persist," *Wall Street Journal* (March 19, 1982), p. 14.

30. Hobart Rowen, "Philippine Debt Stunned Leaders," *Washington Post* (January 29, 1984), p. G18.

31. Irwin L. Kellner, "The Manufacturers Hanover Economic Report" (September 1982), p. 4.

32. Peter Rodgers, "Sweating on the Debts," *Guardian* (June 29, 1984), p. 16.

33. Rowen, "Philippine Debt Stunned Leaders," p. G18.

34. Lindley H. Clark, Jr., "What the Fed Is Up To: The View from Richmond," *Wall Street Journal* (July 17, 1984), p. 31.

35. Hobart Rowen, "U.S. Officials Hint at Bigger Gold Auctions," *Washington Post* (October 3, 1979), p. D9.

36. Adam Raphael, "Cabinet of 'Yes' Men," *Observer* (December 9, 1984), p. 5.

37. James L. Rowe, Jr., "How Interest Rates Are Determined," *Washington Post* (May 20, 1984), p. G1.

38. Robert Heilbroner, "Economic Prospects," *New Yorker* (August 29, 1983), p. 67.

39. H. Erich Heinemann, "Paying the Price for the Mighty Dollar," *New York Times* (June 19, 1983), p. 12.

40. "Stateless Money. A New Force on World Economies," *Business Week* (August 21, 1978), p. 80.

41. "Address by Jacques de Larosière before the Economic

and Social Council of the United Nations," Geneva (July 5, 1984), p. 5.

42. For more on this point, see: Howard M. Wachtel, *Labor and the Economy* (New York: Academic Press, 1984), chap. 9.

43. *Guardian* (January 8, 1985), p. 24.

44. Robert A. Bennett, "Should U.S. Banks Receive Bailouts? Continental Rescue Spotlights Issues," *International Herald Tribune* (September 14, 1984), p. 11; and "William M. Isaac: Despite Failures, Bank Prospects Aren't Bleak," *Washington Post* (July 15, 1984), p. G4.

45. Kenneth B. Noble, "Banking Problems Growing," *International Herald Tribune* (October 22, 1984), p. 7.

46. Michael J. Boskin, "Going Overboard on Bank Bailouts," *Wall Street Journal* (August 23, 1984), p. 22 (emphasis in original).

47. G. Christian Hill and Edward A. Finn, "Big Depositors' Runs on Beleaguered Banks Speed the Failure Rate," *Wall Street Journal* (August 23, 1984), p. 1.

48. Ibid., p. 19.

49. U.S. House of Representatives, *Financial Institutions*, pp. 909–13.

50. "A Banking Rift Over Iran's Assets," *Business Week* (December 10, 1979), p. 30.

51. "Angry Arabs Stay With the Dollar," *Business Week* (December 10, 1979), p. 31.

52. Karin Lissakers, "Money and Manipulation," *Foreign Policy*, 44 (Fall 1981), p. 115.

53. Ibid.

54. "A Banking Rift," p. 30; and "More Iranian Fallout Hits the Euromarket," *Business Week* (December 17, 1979), p. 30.

55. "More Iranian Fallout," p. 30.

56. Anthony Sampson, *The Money Lenders. The People and Politics of the World Banking Crisis* (London: Penguin Books, 1981), p. 312.

57. Ibid., p. 315.

58. Jimmy Carter, *Keeping Faith. Memoirs of a President* (New York: Bantam Books, 1982), p. 4.

59. Lissakers, "Money and Manipulation," p. 119.

60. Carter, *Keeping Faith*, p. 6.

61. Lissakers, "Money and Manipulation," p. 120.

62. Carter, *Keeping Faith*, p. 8.

63. Taken from ibid., pp. 9–13.

64. Ibid., p. 13; and Lissakers, "Money and Manipulation," p. 120.

65. Lissakers, "Money and Manipulation," p. 117.

66. Ibid., p. 115.

67. Ibid., p. 116.

68. John M. Berry, "Banks in Turmoil: Can the System Sustain Shocks," *Washington Post* (May 27, 1984), p. F1.

69. James L. Rowe, Jr., "The Grapevine That Caught Continental," *Washington Post* (May 27, 1984), p. F5.

70. Ibid.

71. Berry, "Banks in Turmoil," p. F1.

72. James L. Rowe, Jr., "U.S., Continental in Accord on Rescue of Chicago Bank," *Washington Post* (July 24, 1984), p. A1.

73. "Possible Nationalizing of Continental Illinois Raises Many Questions," *Wall Street Journal* (July 18, 1984), p. 13.

74. Ibid.

75. Hobart Rowen, "Where Were the Bank Regulators?," *Washington Post* (May 27, 1984), p. F3.

76. Nancy L. Ross, "At Least 5 Potential Partners Courting Continental Illinois," *Washington Post* (May 22, 1984), p. C1.

77. Gipson, "Imprudent Bankers," p. F7.

78. "Possible Nationalization," p. 13.

79. John Updike, *The Coup* (New York: Alfred A. Knopf, 1978), p. 267.

80. James L. Rowe, Jr., "Argentine Loans' Effect Limited," *Washington Post* (July 20, 1984), p. E1.

81. Howard M. Wachtel and Peter D. Adelsheim, "The Inflationary Impact of Unemployment: Price Markups During Postwar Recessions," U.S. Congress, Joint Economic Committee (1976).

Chapter 7. The New Corporate Money Mandarins

1. Robert B. Reich, "The Next American Frontier," *Atlantic Monthly* (March 1983), p. 50.

2. From the publicity brochure for the film *The Business of America . . .* , California Newsreel (1983).

3. Robert B. Reich, *The Next American Frontier* (London: Penguin Books, 1983), pp. 157–58.

4. Nancy L. Ross, "Panel Hears Debate Over Mergers," *Washington Post* (March 29, 1984), p. B1.

5. "Deconglomerating Business," *Business Week* (August 24, 1981), p. 126.

6. Barry Bluestone and Bennett Harrison, *The De-Industrialization of America* (New York: Basic Books, 1982), p. 6.

7. William J. Abernathy, Kim B. Clark, and Alan M. Kantrow, *Industrial Renaissance. Producing a Competitive Future for America* (New York: Basic Books, 1983), p. 8.

8. Ibid.

9. "Dollar Fever Infects the World," *Business Week* (June 27, 1983), p. 94.

10. "America's Restructured Economy," *Business Week* (June 1, 1981), pp. 59–60.

11. Statistics in this paragraph are taken from: Howard M. Wachtel, *Labor and the Economy* (New York: Academic Press, 1984), pp. 15, 16, 383.

12. Committee on Energy and Commerce, U.S. House of Representatives, *The United States in a Changing World Economy: The Case for an Integrated Domestic and International Commercial Policy* (Washington: Government Printing Office, 1983), p. 9.

13. "The Reindustrialization of America," *Business Week* (June 30, 1980), p. 57.

14. Ibid. and Council of Economic Advisers, *Economic Report of the President 1984* (Washington: Government Printing Office, 1984), p. 331.

15. Mohsin Ali, "U.S. Trade Deficit at $123bn," *Times* (January 31, 1985), p. 15.

16. "Dollar Fever Infects the World," pp. 90–91.

17. Ibid., p. 92.

18. Ibid., p. 96.

19. Reich, "The Next American Frontier," pp. 44–45.

20. Ira C. Magaziner and Robert B. Reich, *Minding America's Business. The Decline and Rise of the American Economy* (New York: Vintage Books, 1983), p. 31.

21. "Blueprint for a Comeback," *Industry Week* (June 14, 1982), p. 215.

22. Ralph Kozlow, "Capital Expenditures by Majority-Owned Foreign Affiliates of U.S. Companies, 1984," *Survey of Current Business*, 64, 3 (March 1984), p. 33.

23. Committee on Energy and Commerce, *The United States in a Changing World Economy*, p. 5.

24. Ibid., p. 14.

25. " 'Made in U.S.A.' Means Little to the Multinationals," *Business Week* (April 10, 1978), p. 60.

26. "The Reindustrialization of America," p. 70.

27. Robert H. Hayes and William J. Abernathy, "Managing Our Way to Economic Decline," *Harvard Business Review* (July–August 1980), p. 70.

28. Peter Behr, "Playing It Safe, and Losing Out," *Washington Post* (January 17, 1982), p. A12.

29. Robert Walters, "Who's to Blame for Business Declines?," *Knoxville News-Sentinel* (March 4, 1981), p. D-2.

30. Peter Behr, "Serving Only the Present," *Washington Post* (January 20, 1982), p. D10.

31. Ibid.

32. Ibid.

33. William H. Jones, "Key Executives 'Chuck It' for Career Changes," *Washington Post* (August 3, 1981), p. 17.

34. Michael Maccoby, *The Gamesman. The New Corporate Leaders* (New York: Simon and Schuster, 1976), p. 48.

35. Hayes and Abernathy, "Managing Our Way to Economic Decline," p. 74.

36. "Managing America's Business," *Economist* (December 22, 1984), p. 93.

37. Reich, "The Next American Frontier," p. 58.

38. Gerald R. Rosen, "Pushing Productivity," *Dun's Review* (July 1981), p. 39

39. Behr, "Playing It Safe, and Losing Out," p. A12; and

Hayes and Abernathy, "Managing Our Way to Economic Decline," p. 75.

40. Reich, "The Next American Frontier," p. 58.

41. "Quality: The U.S. Drives to Catch Up," *Business Week* (November 1, 1982), p. 67.

42. Yoshi Tsurumi, " . . . And the Incompetent Americans," *Washington Post* (July 31, 1983), p. D5.

43. Hayes and Abernathy, "Managing Our Way to Economic Decline," p. 74.

44. Mark Green, "The Problem With Business, Says Business, Is Business," *Washington Post* (May 10, 1981), p. B4.

45. Ibid.

46. Robert J. Samuelson, "Can Any Good Come From Merger Turmoil?" *Washington Post* (June 20, 1984), p. F6.

47. "The Reindustrialization of America," p. 81.

48. Arthur Burck, "The Hidden Trauma of Merger Mania," *Business Week* (December 6, 1982), p. 14.

49. "The Reindustrialization of America," p. 78.

50. John Perham, "What CEOs Think of Takeovers," *Dun's Business Month* (November 1983), p. 82.

51. "Merger Boom Can Lead to 'Dinosaur' Companies," *U.S. News & World Report* (December 21, 1981), p. 64.

52. "How the New Merger Boom Will Benefit the Economy," *Business Week* (February 6, 1984), p. 42.

53. Ibid.

54. Ibid., p. 46.

55. Harry Anderson and Connie Leslie, "The Marriage Brokers," *Newsweek* (July 27, 1981), p. 52.

56. Patricia M. Scherschel and Joseph Benham, "Battles Heat up in Takeover Wars," *U.S. News & World Report* (December 21, 1981), p. 63.

57. John Greenwald, "Swallowing Up One Another," *Time* (February 6, 1984), p. 47.

58. Ibid., p. 48.

59. Scherschel and Benham, "Battles Heat Up," p. 64.

60. James L. Rowe Jr., "Big Borrowing Stirs Debate in High Finance," *Washington Post* (March 11, 1984), p. H1.

61. "An Angry Reuss Hits Fund Tieup in Bendix Wars," *Washington Post* (October 3, 1982), P. A16.

62. Mark Potts, "Cement Unit Up for Sale by Marietta," *Washington Post* (January 5, 1983), p. D1.

63. Burck, "The Hidden Trauma of Merger Mania," p. 14.

64. Thomas J. Murray, "Do Mergers Make Sense?," *Dun's Business Month* (October 1982), pp. 88–89.

65. Monica Langley, "Several Strategies Used in Mergers May Be Casualties of Tax Measures" *Wall Street Journal* (July 17, 1984), p. 33.

66. Burck, "The Hidden Trauma of Merger Mania," p. 14.

67. Adrian Hamilton, "New Dawn for Mega-Projects," *Observer* (December 16, 1984), p. 25.

Chapter 8. What's Left? Political Economy in the Supranational Era

1. Robert Heilbroner, "Inflationary Capitalism," *New Yorker* (October 8, 1979), p. 137.

2. "The Year Things Changed," *Economist* (December 22, 1984), p. 49.

3. Ibid., p. 51.

4. William Greider, "The Education of David Stockman," *Atlantic Monthly* (December 1981), p. 46.

5. Vermont Royster, "The Point of It All," *Wall Street Journal* (October 1, 1980), p. 32.

6. Mancur Olson, *The Rise and Decline of Nations. Economic Growth, Stagflation, and Social Rigidities* (New Haven: Yale University Press, 1982), P. 177.

7. Robert J. Samuelson, "Europe's Elusive Prosperity," *Washington Post* (March 29, 1983), p. C1.

8. Michael Walzer, *Spheres of Justice. A Defense of Pluralism and Equality* (New York: Basic Books, 1983), p. 14.

9. Daniel Bell, *The Cultural Contradictions of Capitalism* (New York: Basic Books, 1976).

10. Greider, "The Education of David Stockman," p. 30.

11. Olson, *The Rise and Decline of Nations*, pp. 44, 47.

12. John W. Gardner, *Toward a Pluralistic But Coherent Society* (New York: Aspen Institute for Humanistic Studies, 1980), p. 15.

13. Fred Hirsch, *Social Limits to Growth* (Cambridge: Harvard University Press, 1976), p. 11.

14. Lester C. Thurow, "Equity, Efficiency, Social Justice, and Redistribution," *The Welfare State in Crisis* (Paris: Organization for Economic Cooperation and Development, 1981), p. 147.

15. Everett Carll Ladd, Jr., "What the Voters Really Want," *Fortune* (December 18, 1978), p. 44.

16. "A Call for Tougher—Not Weaker—Antipollution Laws," *Business Week* (January 24, 1983), p. 87.

17. Lloyd A. Free and Hadley Cantril, *The Political Beliefs of Americans. A Study of Public Opinion* (New Brunswick: Rutgers University Press, 1967), pp. 32, 33.

18. Ibid., p. 36.

19. Albert O. Hirschman, *Shifting Involvements. Private Interest and Public Action* (Princeton: Princeton University Press, 1982), p. 132.

20. Ibid., p. 67.

21. Hirsch, *Social Limits to Growth*, p. 92.

22. Ibid., p. 40.

23. Ibid., p. 26.

Chapter 9. Public Policy for a Supranational Order

1. Robert Heilbroner, "Economic Prospects," *New Yorker* (August 29, 1983), p. 72.

2. Ibid., p. 77.

3. Committee on Energy and Commerce, U.S. House of Representatives, *The United States in a Changing World Economy: The Case for an Integrated Domestic and International Commercial Policy* (Washington: Government Printing Office, 1983), p. 18.

4. Fred Hirsch, *Social Limits to Growth* (Cambridge: Harvard University Press, 1976), p. 118.

5. William Keegan, "A *Real* Jobs Budget," *Observer* (March 17, 1985), p. 34.

6. "Superdollar Overdoes It," *Economist* (March 2, 1985), p. 11

7. Summarized in: American Express, *The AMEX Bank Review*, II, 5 (June 19, 1984), pp. 5–7.

8. Felix G. Rohatyn, *The Twenty-Year Century. Essays on Economics and Public Finance* (New York: Random House, 1983), p.61.

9. Committee on Energy and Commerce, *The United States in a Changing World Economy*, pp. 16, 48.

10. Hirsch, *Social Limits to Growth*, p. 135 (emphasis in original).

11. Ibid., pp. 117, 121.

12. Committee on Energy and Commerce, *The United States in a Changing World Economy*, p. 41.

13. Robert D. Putnam and Nicholas Bayne, *Hanging Together. The Seven-Power Summits* (Cambridge: Harvard University Press, 1984), p. 14.

14. Committee on Energy and Commerce, *The United States in a Changing World Economy*, p. 18.

15. Helmut Schmidt and Manfred Lahnstein, "The World Economy at Stake," *Economist* (February 26, 1983), p. 19.

16. Putnam and Bayne, *Hanging Together*, p. 6.

17. Schmidt and Lahnstein, "The World Economy at Stake," p. 30.

18. Putnam and Bayne, *Hanging Together*, p. 3.

19. For example, see the proposals in: *Towards a New Bretton Woods. Challenges for the World Financial and Trading System* (London: Commonwealth Secretariat, 1983).

INDEX

Abernathy, William J., 157, 163–4, 166, 167
Acheson, Dean, 25
Agee, William, 172–3
agriculture, 9–10
Algeria, 74, 105, 144, 145
Aliber, Robert Z. 103
American Bankers Assoc., 42–3
American Broadcasting Co., 170
Anaconda Copper Corp., 5–6
Anderson, J. W., 9, 20
anti-Semitism, 27
antitrust regulation, 133, 176
Argentina, 124, 131, 151, 175
austerity programs, xii, 4, 12, 118, 119, 121–2, 150–2, 183, 204, 205, 207, 212, 224–5; creative-destruction process, 122; IMF program, 127–30; paradoxes of, 129; rises in interest rates and, 151–2, 212
Australia, 28, 77
automobile industry, 156, 161

Bahama Is., 110–11, 112, 114, 141, 142
Bailey, Norman A., 124, 127
balance of payments, 32, 37; dollar outflow (1950s), 60–1, 97–8; Kennedy programs, 66–7, 69–72; Johnson policies, 73, 77; and Viet Nam, 75–9; dollar outflow (1970–71), 80–2, 83, 84; IMF regimen for, 128
balance of trade, 30, 159; and foreign exchange rates, 47, 49, 50; under Bretton Woods, 53, 54, 60, 61, 66; Johnson's export loan programs, 77; Nixon's import surcharge, 84, 85; U.S. deficit, 160
bancor (currency unit), 48, 51, 78
Bani-Sadr, Abolhassan, 140, 141
Bank Markazi, 144
Bank of America, 143
Bank of England, 52
Bank for International Settlements (BIS), 100–1, 122
Bankhaus Herstatt, 139, 140
banks, bankers, xiii, 3, 5, 7, 26, 148; federal bailouts, 17, 19, 138–9, 148–9, 206; vs. Bretton Woods

agreements, 42–3; vs. foreign exchange controls, 77; reserve requirements, 102–3; and Third World loans, 107–8, 123, 124, 131, 150–2; foreign branches, 112–15; overnight lending, 113–14, 146; foreign exchange transactions, 114–15, 133, 139–40; free-trade zones, 116–18; loss of credibility, 131, 206–7; vs. antitrust regulations, 133; and Iranian asset freeze, 140, 142–6. *See also* international banking system; offshore banking
Banque Commerciale pour l'Europe du Nord, 94
Banque de France, 74, 76
Barnet, Richard, 6
barter economy, 30
Basel Agreement (1961), 70
Baskin, Michael J., 139
Baucus, Sen. Max, 6
Bayne, Nicholas, 216, 222
Behn, Aphra, 32
Behr, Peter, 165
Belgrade Conference (1979), 132–5
Bell, Daniel, 194
Bendix Corp., 173
Bentley, Elizabeth, 56
Bergsten, C. Fred, 11
Bernstein, Edward, 23, 27
black workers, 189
Bluestone, Barry, 156
Bolivia, 124
Booth, Charles, 186
Bradley, Sen. William, 129
Brazil, 107, 124, 131, 159, 175
Bretton Woods Conference (1944), 23–8, 39–40, 41, 57–8, 196
Bretton Woods system, xii, 32, 68, 119, 120, 195, 218; collapse of, 2–3, 9, 11, 15–17, 84–6, 104, 159, 183, 207, 216; fixed-exchange-rate principle, 24, 46–51, 54; internationalism vs. U.S. economic superiority, 34–6; conservative opposition to, 42–3; and gold standard, 46–7, 51–2, 61, 75; as stabilizing mechanism, 48–52; economic and political benefits to U.S., 52–5, 56; and postwar reconstruction, 60–1; fail-safe mechanism, 62, 64–5; and Nixon's policies 79, 84; need for second, 224